I0764392

IN THE ROCKY MOUNTAINS

W. H. G. KINGSTON

In the Rocky Mountains

W. H. G. Kingston

PO Box 2211
Fairfield, IA 52556
www.1stworldlibrary.com
First Edition

LCCN: 2007930934

Softcover ISBN: 978-1-4218-4870-9
Hardcover ISBN: 978-1-4218-4773-3
eBook ISBN: 978-1-4218-4967-6

1st World Library Literary Society

Giving Back to the World

"If you want to work on the core problem, it's early school literacy."

- James Barksdale, former CEO of Netscape

"No skill is more crucial to the future of a child, or to a democratic and prosperous society, than literacy."

- Los Angeles Times

"Literacy... means far more than learning how to read and write... The aim is to transmit... knowledge and promote social participation."

- UNESCO

"Literacy is not a luxury, it is a right and a responsibility. If our world is to meet the challenges of the twenty-first century we must harness the energy and creativity of all our citizens."

- President Bill Clinton

"Parents should be encouraged to read to their children, and teachers should be equipped with all available techniques for teaching literacy, so the varying needs and capacities of individual kids can be taken into account."

- Hugh Mackay

CHAPTER ONE

HOW UNCLE JEFF CAME TO "ROARING WATER"—THE SITUATION OF THE FARM—THE INMATES OF THE HOUSE—MY SISTER CLARICE AND BLACK RACHEL—UNCLE JEFF—BARTLE WON AND GIDEON TUTTLE—ARRIVAL OF LIEUTENANT BROADSTREET AND HIS MEN—THE TROOPERS QUARTERED IN THE HUT—OUR FARM-LABOURERS—SUDDEN APPEARANCE OF THE REDSKIN WINNEMAK—HIS FORMER VISIT TO THE FARM—CLARICE ENCOUNTERS HIM AT THE SPRING—BADLY WOUNDED—KINDLY TREATED BY CLARICE AND RACHEL—HIS GRATITUDE.

We were most of us seated round a blazing fire of pine logs, which crackled away merrily, sending the sparks about in all directions, at the no small risk of setting fire to garments of a lighter texture than ours. Although the flowers were blooming on the hill-sides, in the woods and valleys, and by the margins of the streams; humming-birds were flitting about gathering their dainty food; and the bears, having finished the operation of licking their paws, had come out in search of more substantial fare; and the buffalo had been seen migrating to the north,—the wind at night blew keenly from off the snow-capped mountain-tops which, at no great distance, rose above us, and rendered a fire acceptable even to us hardy backwoodsmen.

Our location was far in advance of any settlement in that latitude of North America, for Uncle Jeff Crockett "could never abide," he averred, "being in the rear of his fellow-creatures." Whenever he had before found people gathering around him at the spot where he had pitched his tent, or rather, put up his log-hut, he had sold his property (always to advantage, however), and yoking his team, had pushed on westward, with a few sturdy followers.

On and on he had come, until he had reached the base of the Rocky Mountains. He would have gone over them, but, having an eye to business, and knowing that it was necessary to secure a market for his produce, he calculated that he had come far enough for the present. He therefore climbed the sides of the mountain for a short distance, until he entered a sort of canon, which, penetrating westward, greatly narrowed, until it had the appearance of a cleft with lofty crags on either side,—while it opened out eastward, over-looking the broad valley and the plain beyond.

He chose the spot as one capable of being defended against the Redskins, never in those parts very friendly to white men,—especially towards those whom they found settling themselves on lands which they looked upon as their own hunting-grounds, although they could use them for no other purpose.

Another reason which had induced Uncle Jeff to select this spot was, that not far off was one of the only practicable passes through the mountains either to the north or south, and that the trail to it led close below us at the foot of the hills, so that every emigrant train or party of travellers going to or from the Great Salt Lake or California must pass in sight of the house.

A stream, issuing from the heights above, fell over the cliffs, forming a roaring cataract; and then, rushing through the canon, made its way down into the valley, irrigating and fertilising the ground, until it finally reached a large river, the Platte, flowing into the Missouri. From this cataract our location obtained its name of "Roaring Water;" but it was equally well-known as "Uncle Jeff's Farm."

Our neighbours, if such they could be called in this wild region, were "birds of passage." Now and then a few Indian families might fix their tents in the valley below; or a party of hunters or trappers might bivouac a night or two under the shelter of the woods, scattered here and there; or travellers bound east or west might encamp by the margin of the river for the sake of recruiting their cattle, or might occasionally seek for shelter at the log-house which they saw perched above them, where, in addition to comfortable quarters, abundant fare and a hospitable welcome—which Uncle Jeff never refused to any one, whoever he might be, who came to his door—were sure to be obtained.

But it is time that I should say something about the inmates of the house at the period I am describing.

First, there was Uncle Jeff Crockett, a man of about forty-five, with a tall, stalwart figure, and a handsome countenance (though scarred by a slash from a tomahawk, and the claws of a bear with which he had had a desperate encounter). A bright blue eye betokened a keen sight, as also that his rifle was never likely to miss its aim; while his well-knit frame gave assurance of great activity and endurance.

I was then about seventeen, and Uncle Jeff had more than once complimented me by remarking that "I was a true chip of the old block," as like what he was when at my age as two peas, and that he had no fear but that I should do him credit; so that I need not say any more about myself.

I must say something, however, about my sister Clarice, who was my junior by rather more than a year. Fair as a lily she was, in spite of summer suns, from which she took but little pains to shelter herself; but they had failed even to freckle her clear skin, or darken her light hair—except, it might be, that from them it obtained the golden hue which tinged it. Delicate as she looked, she took an active part in all household duties, and was now busy about some of them at the further end of the big hall, which served as our common sitting-room, workshop, kitchen, and often as a sleeping-room, when guests were numerous. She was assisted by Rachel Prentiss, a middle-aged negress, the only other woman in the establishment; who took upon herself the out-door work and rougher duties, with the exception of tending the poultry and milking the cows, in which Clarice also engaged.

I have not yet described the rest of the party round the fire. There was Bartle Won, a faithful follower, for many years, of Uncle Jeff; but as unlike him as it was possible that any two human beings could be. Bartle was a wiry little fellow, with bow legs, broad shoulders (one rather higher than the other), and a big head, out of which shone a pair of grey eyes, keen as those of a hawk—the only point in which he resembled Uncle Jeff. He was wonderfully active and strong, notwithstanding his figure; and as for fatigue, he did not know what it meant. He could go days without eating or drinking; although, when he did get food, he certainly made ample amends for his abstinence. He was no great runner; but when once on the back of a horse, no animal, however vicious and up to tricks, had been able to dislodge him.

Gideon Tuttle was another faithful follower of Uncle Jeff: he was a hardy backwoodsman, whose gleaming axe had laid many monarchs of the forest low. Though only of moderate height, few men could equal him in strength. He could fell an ox with his fist, and hold down by the horns a young bull, however furious. He had had several encounters with bears; and although on two occasions only armed with a knife, he had come off victorious. His nerve and activity equalled his strength. He was no great talker, and he was frequently morose and ill-tempered; but he had one qualification which compensated for all his other deficiencies—he was devotedly attached to Uncle Jeff.

There were engaged on the farm, besides these, four other hands: an Irishman, a Spaniard, a negro, and a half-breed, who lived by themselves in a rough hut near the house. Although Uncle Jeff was a great advocate for liberty and equality, he had no fancy to have these fellows in-doors; their habits and language not being such as to make close intimacy pleasant.

The two old followers of Uncle Jeff—although they would have laughed at the notion of being called gentlemen—were clean in their persons, and careful in their conversation, especially in the presence of Clarice.

Just before sunset that evening, our party had been increased by the arrival of an officer of the United States army and four men, who were on their way from Fort Laramie to Fort Harwood, on the other side of the mountains; but they had been deserted by their Indian guide, and having been unable to find the entrance to the pass, were well-nigh worn out with fatigue and vexation when they caught sight of Roaring Water Farm.

The officer and his men were received with a hearty welcome.

"There is food enough in the store, and we will make a shake-down for you in this room," said Uncle Jeff, wringing the hand of the officer in his usual style.

The latter introduced himself as Lieutenant Manley Broadstreet. He was a fine-looking young fellow, scarcely older than I was; but he had already seen a great deal of service in border warfare with the Indians, as well as in Florida and Texas.

"You are welcome here, friends," said Uncle Jeff, who, as I have said, was no respecter of persons, and made little distinction between the lieutenant and his men.

At this Lieutenant Broadstreet demurred, and, as he glanced at Clarice, inquired whether there was any building near in which the men could be lodged.

"They are not very fit company for a young lady," he remarked aside.

He did not, however, object to the sergeant joining him; and the other three men were accordingly ordered to take up their quarters at the hut, with its motley inhabitants.

Their appearance, I confess, somewhat reminded me of Falstaff's "ragged regiment." The three varied wonderfully in height. The tallest was not only tall, but thin in the extreme, his ankles protruding below his trousers, and his wrists beyond the sleeves of his jacket; he had lost his military hat, and had substituted for it a high beaver, which he had obtained from some Irish emigrant on the road. He was a German; and his name, he told me, was Karl Klitz. The shortest of the party, Barnaby Gillooly, was also by far the fattest; indeed, it seemed surprising that, with his obese figure, he could undergo the fatigue he must constantly have been called upon to endure. He seemed to be a jolly, merry fellow notwithstanding, as he showed by breaking into a hearty laugh as Klitz, stumbling over a log, fell with his long neck and shoulders on the one side, and his heels kicking up in the air on the other. The last man was evidently a son of Erin, from the few words he uttered in a rich brogue, which had not deteriorated by long absence from home and country. He certainly presented a more soldierly appearance than did his two comrades, but the ruddy blue hue of his nose and lips showed that when liquor was to be obtained he was not likely to let it pass his lips untasted.

The three soldiers were welcomed by the inhabitants of the hut, who were glad to have strangers with whom they could chat, and who could bring them news from the Eastern States.

On coming back to the house, after conducting the three men to the hut, I found the lieutenant and his sergeant, Silas Custis, seated before the fire; the young lieutenant every now and then, as was not surprising, casting a glance at Clarice. But she was too busily occupied in getting the supper-table ready to notice the admiration she was inspiring.

Rachel, with frying-pan in hand, now made her way towards the fire, and begging those who impeded her movements to draw on one side, she commenced her culinary operations. She soon had a huge dish of rashers of bacon ready; while a couple of pots were carried off to be emptied of their contents; and some cakes, which had been cooking under the ashes, were withdrawn, and placed hot and smoking on the platter.

"All ready, genl'em," exclaimed Rachel; "you can fall to when you like."

The party got up, and we took our seats at the table. Clarice, who until a short time before had been assisting Rachel, now returned—having been away to arrange her toilet. She took her usual seat at the head of the table; and the lieutenant, to his evident satisfaction, found himself placed near her. He spoke in a pleasant, gentlemanly tone, and treated Clarice in every respect as a young lady,—as, indeed, she was. He now and then addressed me; and the more he said, the more I felt inclined to like him.

Uncle Jeff had a good deal of conversation with Sergeant Custis, who appeared to be a superior sort of person, and had, I suspect, seen better days.

We were still seated at supper when the door opened and an Indian stalked into the room, decked with war-paint and feathers, and rifle in hand.

"Ugh!" he exclaimed, stopping and regarding us, as if unwilling to advance without permission.

"Come in, friend," said Uncle Jeff, rising and going towards him; "sit down, and make yourself at home. You would like some food, I guess?"

The Indian again uttered a significant "Ugh!" as, taking advantage of Uncle Jeff's offer, he seated himself by the fire.

"Why, uncle," exclaimed Clarice, "it is Winnemak!"

* * * * *

But I must explain how Clarice came to know the Indian, whom, at the first moment, no one else had recognised.

Not far off, in a grove of cottonwood trees up the valley,

there came forth from the side of the hill a spring of singularly bright and cool water, of which Uncle Jeff was particularly fond; as were, indeed, the rest of us. Clarice made it a practice every evening, just before we returned home from our day's work, to fetch a large pitcher of water from this spring, that we might have it as cool and fresh as possible.

It happened that one afternoon, in the spring of the previous year, she had set off with this object in view, telling Rachel where she was going; but she had just got out of the enclosure when she caught sight of one of the cows straying up the valley.

"I go after her, Missie Clarice; you no trouble you-self," cried Rachel.

So Clarice continued her way, carrying her pitcher on her head. It was somewhat earlier than usual; and having no especial work to attend to at home, she did not hurry. It was as warm a day as any in summer, and finding the heat somewhat oppressive, she sat down by the side of the pool to enjoy the refreshing coolness of the air which came down the canon. "I ought to be going home," she said to herself; and taking her pitcher, she filled it with water.

She was just about to replace it on her head, when she was startled by the well-known Indian "Ugh!" uttered by some one who was as yet invisible. She at first felt a little alarmed, but recollecting that if the stranger had been an enemy he would not have given her warning, she stood still, with her pitcher in her hand, looking around her. Presently an Indian appeared from among the bushes, his dress torn and travel-stained, and his haggard looks showing that he must have undergone great fatigue. He made signs, as he approached, to show that he had come over the mountains; he then pointed to his lips, to let her understand that he was parched with thirst.

"Poor man! you shall have some water, then," said Clarice, immediately holding up the pitcher, that the stranger might drink without difficulty. His looks brightened as she did so; and after he had drunk his fill he gave her back the pitcher, drawing a long breath, and placing his hand on his heart to express his gratitude.

While the Indian was drinking, Clarice observed Rachel approaching, with a look of alarm on her countenance. It vanished, however, when she saw how Clarice and the Indian were employed.

"Me dare say de stranger would like food as well as drink," she observed as she joined them, and making signs to the Indian to inquire if he was hungry.

He nodded his head, and uttered some words. But although neither Clarice nor Rachel could understand his language, they saw very clearly that he greatly required food.

"Come along, den," said Rachel; "you shall hab some in de twinkle ob an eye, as soon as we get home.—Missie Clarice, me carry de pitcher, or Indian fancy you white slavey;" and Rachel laughed at her own wit.

She then told Clarice how she had caught sight of the Indian coming over the mountain, as she was driving home the cow; and that, as he was making his way towards the spring, she had been dreadfully alarmed at the idea that he might surprise her young mistress. She thought it possible, too, that he might be accompanied by other Redskins, and that they should perhaps carry her off; or, at all events, finding the house undefended, they might pillage it, and get away with their booty before the return of the men.

"But he seems friendly and well-disposed," said Clarice, looking at the Indian; "and even if he had not been suffering from hunger and thirst, I do not think he would have been inclined to do us any harm. The Redskins are not all bad; and many, I fear, have been driven, by the ill treatment they have received from white men, to retaliate, and have obtained a worse character than they deserve."

"Dere are bad red men, and bad white men, and bad black men; but, me tink, not so many ob de last," said Rachel, who always stuck up for her own race.

The red man seemed to fancy that they were talking about him; and he tried to smile, but failed in the attempt. It was with difficulty, too, he could drag on his weary limbs.

As soon as they reached the house Rachel made him sit down; and within a minute or two a basin of broth was placed before him, at which she blew away until her cheeks almost cracked, in an endeavour to cool it, that he might the more speedily set to. He assisted her, as far as his strength would allow, in the operation; and then placing the basin to his lips, he eagerly drained off its contents, without making use of the wooden spoon with which she had supplied him.

"Dat just to keep body and soul togedder, till somet'ing more 'stantial ready for you," she said.

Clarice had in the meantime been preparing some venison steaks, which, with some cakes from the oven, were devoured by the Indian with the same avidity with which he had swallowed the broth. But although the food considerably revived him, he still showed evident signs of exhaustion; so Rachel, placing a buffalo robe in the corner of the room, invited him to lie down and rest. He staggered towards it, and in a few minutes his heavy breathing showed that he was asleep.

Uncle Jeff was somewhat astonished, when he came in, on seeing the Indian; but he approved perfectly of what Clarice and Rachel had done.

"To my mind," he observed, "when these Redskins choose to be enemies, we must treat them as enemies, and shoot them down, or they will be having our scalps; but if they wish to be friends, we should treat them as friends, and do them all the good we can."

Uncle Jeff forgot just then that we ought to do good to our enemies as well as to our friends; but that would be a difficult matter for a man to accomplish when a horde of savages are in arms, resolved to take his life; so I suppose it means that we must do them good when we can get them to be at peace—or to bury the war-hatchet, as they would express themselves.

The Indian slept on, although he groaned occasionally as if in pain,—nature then asserting its sway, though, had he been awake, he probably would have given no sign of what he was suffering.

"I suspect the man must be wounded," observed Uncle Jeff. "It will be better not to disturb him."

We had had supper, and the things were being cleared away, when, on going to look at the Indian, I saw that his eyes were open, and that he was gazing round him, astonished at seeing so many people.

"He is awake," I observed; and Clarice, coming up, made

signs to inquire whether he would have some more food.

He shook his head, and lay back again, evidently unable to sit up.

Just then Uncle Jeff, who had been out, returned.

"I suspect that he is one of the Kaskayas, whose hunting-grounds are between this and the Platte," observed Uncle Jeff; and approaching the Indian, he stooped over him and spoke a few words in the dialect of the tribe he had mentioned.

The Indian answered him, although with difficulty.

"I thought so," said Uncle Jeff. "He has been badly wounded by an arrow in the side, and although he managed to cut it out and bind up the hurt, he confesses that he still suffers greatly. Here, Bartle, you are the best doctor among us," he added, turning to Won, who was at work mending some harness on the opposite side of the room; "see what you can do for the poor fellow."

Bartle put down the straps upon which he was engaged, and joined us, while Clarice retired. Uncle Jeff and Bartle then examined the Indian's side.

"I will get some leaves to bind over the wound to-morrow morning, which will quickly heal it; and, in the meantime, we will see if Rachel has not got some of the ointment which helped to cure Gideon when he cut himself so badly with his axe last spring."

Rachel, who prided herself on her ointment, quickly produced a jar of it, and assisted Bartle in dressing the Indian's wound. She then gave him a cooling mixture which she had concocted.

The Indian expressed his gratitude in a few words, and again covering himself up with a buffalo robe, was soon asleep.

The next morning he was better, but still unable to move.

He remained with us ten days, during which Clarice and Rachel watched over him with the greatest care, making him all sorts of dainty dishes which they thought he would like; and in that time he and Uncle Jeff managed to understand each other pretty well.

The Indian, according to the reticent habits of his people, was not inclined to be very communicative at first as to how he had received his wound; but as his confidence increased he owned that he had, with a party of his braves, made an excursion to the southward to attack their old enemies the Arrapahas, but that he and his followers had been overwhelmed by greatly superior numbers. His people had been cut off to a man, and himself badly wounded. He had managed, however, to make his escape to the mountains without being observed by his foes. As he knew that they were on the watch for him, he was afraid of returning to the plains, and had kept on the higher ground, where he had suffered greatly from hunger and thirst, until he had at length fallen in with Clarice at the spring.

At last he was able to move about; and his wound having completely healed, he expressed his wish to return to his people.

"Winnemak will ever be grateful for the kindness shown him by the Palefaces," he said, as he was wishing us good-bye. "A time may come when he may be able to show what he feels; he is one who never forgets his friends, although he may be far away from them."

"We shall be happy to see you whenever you come this way," said Uncle Jeff; "but as for doing us any good, why, we do not exactly expect that. We took care of you, as we should take care of any one who happened to be in distress and wanted assistance, whether a Paleface or a Redskin."

Winnemak now went round among us, shaking each person by the hand. When he came to Clarice he stopped, and spoke to her for some time,—although, of course, she could not understand a word he said.

Uncle Jeff, who was near, made out that he was telling her he had a daughter of her age, and that he should very much like to make them known to each other. "My child is called Maysotta, the 'White Lily;' though, when she sees you, she will say that that name ought to be yours," he added.

Clarice asked Uncle Jeff to tell Winnemak that she should be very glad to become acquainted with Maysotta whenever he could bring her to the farm.

Uncle Jeff was so pleased with the Indian, that he made him a present of a rifle and a stock of ammunition; telling him that he was sure he would ever be ready to use it in the service of his friends.

Winnemak's gratitude knew no bounds, and he expressed himself far more warmly than Indians are accustomed to do. Then bidding us farewell, he took his way to the north-east.

"I know these Indians pretty well," observed Bartle, as Winnemak disappeared in the distance. "We may see his face again when he wants powder and shot, but he will not trouble himself to come back until then."

We had begun to fancy that Bartle was right, for many months went by and we saw nothing of our Indian friend. Our surprise, therefore, was great, when he made his appearance in the manner I have described in an earlier portion of the chapter.

CHAPTER TWO

WINNEMAK WARNS US OF THE APPROACH OF INDIANS—BARTLE GOES OUT TO SCOUT—NO SIGNS OF A FOE—I TAKE THE LIEUTENANT TO VISIT "ROARING WATER"—BARTLE REPORTS THAT THE ENEMY HAVE TURNED BACK—THE LIEUTENANT DELAYED BY THE SERGEANT'S ILLNESS—THE VISIT TO THE HUT—A TIPSY TROOPER—KLITZ AND GILLOOLY MISSING—THE LIEUTENANT BECOMES WORSE—SEARCH FOR THE MISSING MEN—I OFFER TO ACT AS GUIDE TO THE LIEUTENANT—BARTLE UNDERTAKES TO FIND OUT WHAT HAS BECOME OF KLITZ AND BARNEY.

"Glad to see you, friend!" said Uncle Jeff, getting up and taking the Indian by the hand. "What brings you here?"

"To prove that Winnemak has not forgotten the kindness shown him by the Palefaces," was the answer. "He has come to warn his friends, who sleep in security, that their enemies are on the war-path, and will ere long attempt to take their scalps."

"They had better not try that game," said Uncle Jeff; "if they do, they will find that they have made a mistake."

"The Redskins fight not as do the Palefaces; they try to take their enemies by surprise," answered Winnemak. "They will wait until they can find the white men scattered about over the farm, when they will swoop down upon them like the eagle on its prey; or when all are slumbering within, they will creep up to the house, and attack it before there is time for defence."

"Much obliged for your warning, friend," said Uncle Jeff; "but I should like to know more about these enemies, and where they are to be found. We might manage to turn the tables, and be down upon them when they fancy that we are all slumbering in security, and thus put them to the right-about."

"They are approaching as stealthily as the snake in the grass," answered Winnemak. "Unless you can get on their trail, it will be no easy matter to find them."

"Who are these enemies you speak of; and how do you happen to know that they are coming to attack us?" asked Uncle Jeff, who generally suspected all Indian reports, and fancied that Winnemak was merely repeating what he had heard, or, for some reason of his own—perhaps to gain credit to himself—had come to warn us of a danger which had no real existence.

"I was leading forth my braves to revenge the loss we suffered last year, when our scouts brought word that they had fallen in with a large war-party of Arrapahas and Apaches, far too numerous for our small band to encounter with any chance of success. We accordingly retreated, watching for an opportunity to attack any parties of the enemy who might become separated from the larger body. They also sent out their scouts, and one of these we captured. My braves were about to put him to death, but I promised him his liberty if he would tell me the object of the expedition. Being a man who was afraid to die, he told us that the party consisted of his own tribe and the Apaches, who had been joined by some Spanish Palefaces; and that their object was not to make war on either the Kaskayas or the Pawnees, but to rob a wealthy settler living on the side of the mountains, as well as any other white men they might find located in the neighbourhood. Feeling sure that their evil designs were against my friends, I directed my people to follow me, while I hastened forward to give you due warning of what is likely to happen. As they are very numerous, and have among them firearms and ammunition, it may be a hard task, should they attack the house, to beat them off."

Such in substance was the information Winnemak brought us.

"To my mind, the fellows will never dare to come so far north as this; or, if they do, they will think twice about it before they venture to attack our farm," answered Uncle Jeff.

"A wise man is prepared for anything which can possibly happen," said the Indian. "What is there to stop them? They are too numerous to be successfully opposed by any force of white men in these parts; and my braves are not willing to throw away their lives to no purpose."

Uncle Jeff thought the matter over. "I will send out a trusty scout to ascertain who these people are, and what they are about," he said at length. "If they are coming this way, we shall get ready to receive them; and if not, we need not further trouble ourselves."

Lieutenant Broadstreet, who held the Indians cheap, was very much inclined to doubt the truth of the account brought by Winnemak, but he agreed that Uncle Jeff's plan was a prudent one.

Bartle Won immediately volunteered to start off to try and find the whereabouts of the supposed marauding party. His offer was at once accepted; and before many minutes were over he had left the farm, armed with his trusty rifle, and his axe and hunting-knife in his belt.

"Take care they do not catch you," observed the lieutenant.

"If you knew Bartle, you would not give him such advice," said Uncle Jeff. "He is not the boy to be caught napping by Redskins; he is more likely to lay a dozen of them low than lose his own scalp."

The Indian seeing Bartle go, took his leave, saying that he would join his own people, who were to encamp, according to his orders, near a wood in the valley below. He too intended to keep a watch on the enemy; and should he ascertain that they were approaching, he would, he said, give us warning.

"We can trust to your assistance, should we be attacked," said Uncle Jeff; "or, if you will come with your people inside the house, you may help us in defending it."

Winnemak shook his head at the latter proposal.

"We will aid you as far as we can with our small party," he answered; "but my people would never consent to shut themselves up within walls. They do not understand that sort of fighting. Trust to Winnemak; he will do all he can to serve you."

"We are very certain of that, friend," said Uncle Jeff.

The Indian, after once more shaking hands with us, set off to join his tribe.

Lieutenant Broadstreet expressed his satisfaction at having come to the farm. "If you are attacked, my four men and I may be of some use to you; for I feel sure that we shall quickly drive away the Redskins, however numerous they may be," he observed.

He advised that all the doors and lower windows should be barricaded, in case a surprise might be attempted; and that guards should be posted, and another scout sent out to keep watch near the house, in case Bartle might have missed the enemy, or any accident have happened to him. The latter Uncle Jeff deemed very unnecessary, so great was his confidence in Bartle's judgment and activity.

Notice was sent to the hut directing the men to come in should they be required, but it was not considered necessary for them to sleep inside the house.

These arrangements having been made, those not on watch retired to rest. But although Uncle Jeff took things so coolly, I suspect that he was rather more anxious than he wished it to appear. I know that I myself kept awake the greater part of the night, listening for any sounds which might indicate the approach of a foe, and ready to set out at a moment's notice with my rifle in hand,—which I had carefully loaded and placed by my bedside before I lay down. Several times I started up, fancying that I heard a distant murmur; but it was simply the roaring of the cataract coming down the canon.

At daybreak I jumped up, and quickly dressing, went downstairs. Soon afterwards Gideon Tuttle, who had been scouting near the house, came in, stating that he had seen no light to the southward which would indicate the camp-fires of an enemy, and that, according to his belief, none was likely to appear. In this Uncle Jeff was inclined to agree with him.

Lieutenant Broadstreet now expressed a wish to proceed on his way; at the same time, he said that he did not like to leave us until it was certain that we were not likely to be exposed to danger.

"Much obliged to you, friend," said Uncle Jeff, "you are welcome to stay here as long as you please; and Bartle Won will soon be in, when we shall know all about the state of affairs."

It was our custom to breakfast at an early hour in the morning, as we had to be away looking after the cattle, and attending to the other duties of the farm.

The lieutenant happened to ask me why we called the location "Roaring Water."

"I see only a quiet, decent stream flowing by into the valley below," he observed.

"Wait until we have a breeze coming down the canon, and then you will understand why we gave the name of 'Roaring Water' to this place," I answered. "As I can be spared this morning, and there is not much chance of the enemy coming, if you like to accompany me I will take you to the cataract which gives its name to this 'quiet, decent stream,' as you call it; then you will believe that we have not misnamed the locality."

We set off together. The lieutenant looked as if he would have liked to ask Clarice to accompany us; but she was busy about her household duties, and gave no response to his unspoken invitation.

Boy-like, I took a great fancy to the young officer. He was quiet and gentlemanly, and free from all conceit.

I took him to Cold-Water Spring, at which Clarice had met the Indian; and after swallowing a draught from it, we made our way onward over the rough rocks and fallen logs until we came in sight of what we called our cataract. It appeared directly before us, rushing, as it were, out of the side of the hill (though in reality there was a considerable stream above us, which was concealed by the summits of the intervening rocks); then downward it came in two leaps, striking a ledge about half-way, where masses of spray were sent off; and then taking a second leap, it fell into a pool; now rushing forth again foaming and roaring down a steep incline, until it reached the more level portion of the canon.

"That is indeed a fine cataract, and you have well named your location from it," observed the lieutenant. "I wish I had had my sketch-book with me; I might have made a drawing of it, to carry away in remembrance of my visit here."

"I will send you one with great pleasure," I answered.

"Do you draw?" he asked, with a look of surprise, probably thinking that such an art was not likely to be possessed by a young backwoodsman.

"I learned when I was a boy, and I have a taste that way, although I have but little time to exercise it," I answered.

He replied that he should be very much obliged. "Does your sister draw?—I conclude that young lady is your sister?" he said in a tone of inquiry.

"Oh yes! Clarice draws better than I do," I said. "But she has even less time than I have, for she is busy from morning till night; there is no time to spare for amusement of any sort. Uncle Jeff would not approve of our 'idling our time,' as he would call it, in that sort of way."

The lieutenant seemed inclined to linger at the waterfall, so that I had to hurry him away, as I wanted to be back to attend to my duties. I was anxious, also, to hear what account Bartle Won would bring in.

But the day passed away, and Bartle did not appear. Uncle Jeff's confidence that he could have come to no harm was not, however, shaken.

"It may be that he has discovered the enemy, and is watching their movements; or perhaps he has been tempted to go on and on until he has found out that there is no enemy to be met with, or that they have taken the alarm and beat a retreat," he observed.

Still the lieutenant was unwilling to leave us, although Uncle Jeff did not press him to stay.

"It will never do for me to hurry off with my men, and leave a party of whites in a solitary farm to be slaughtered by those Redskin savages," he said.

At all events, he stayed on until the day was so far spent that it would not have been worth while to have started.

Clarice found a little leisure to sit down at the table with her needle-work, very much to the satisfaction of the lieutenant, who did his best to make himself agreeable.

I was away down the valley driving the cattle into their pen, when I caught sight of Bartle coming along at his usual swinging pace towards the farm.

"Well, what news?" I asked, as I came up to him.

"Our friend Winnemak was not romancing," he answered.

"There were fully as many warriors on the war-path as he stated; but, for some reason or other, they turned about and are going south. I came upon their trail after they had broken up their last camp, and I had no difficulty in getting close enough to them to make out their numbers, and the tribes they belong to. The appearance of their camp, however, told me clearly that they are a very large body. We have to thank the chief for his warning; at the same time, we need not trouble ourselves any more on the subject."

"Have they done any harm on their march?" I asked.

"As to that, I am afraid that some settlers to the south have suffered; for I saw, at night, the glare of several fires, with which the rascals must have had something to do. I only hope that the poor white men had time to escape with their lives. If I had not been in a hurry to get back, I would have followed the varmints, and picked off any stragglers I might have come across."

"As you, my friends, are safe for the present, I must be off to-morrow morning with my men," said the lieutenant when I got back; "but I will report the position you are in at Fort Harwood, and should you have reason to expect an attack you can dispatch a messenger, and relief will, I am sure, be immediately sent you."

I do not know that Uncle Jeff cared much about this promise, so confident did he feel in his power to protect his own property,—believing that his men, though few, would prove staunch. But he thanked the lieutenant, and hoped he should have the pleasure of seeing him again before long.

* * * * *

During the night the sergeant was taken ill; and as he was no better in the morning, Lieutenant Broadstreet, who did not wish to go without him, was further delayed. The lieutenant hoped, however, that by noon the poor fellow might have sufficiently recovered to enable them to start.

After breakfast I accompanied him to the hut to visit the other men. Although he summoned them by name,—shouting out "Karl Klitz," "Barney Gillooly," "Pat Sperry,"—no one answered; so, shoving open the door, we entered. At first the hut appeared to be empty, but as we looked into one of the bunks we beheld the last-named individual, so sound asleep that, though his officer shouted to him to know what had become of his comrades, he only replied by grunts.

"The fellow must be drunk," exclaimed the lieutenant, shaking the man.

This was very evident; and as the lieutenant intended not to set off immediately, he resolved to leave him in bed to sleep off his debauch.

But what had become of the German and the fat Irishman? was the question. The men belonging to the hut were all away, so we had to go in search of one of them, to learn if he could give any account of the truants. The negro, who went by no other name than Sam or Black Sam, was the first we met. Sam averred, on his honour as a gentleman, that when he left the hut in the morning they were all sleeping as quietly as lambs; and he concluded that they had gone out to take a bath in the stream, or a draught of cool water at the spring. The latter the lieutenant thought most probable, if they had been indulging in potations of whisky on the previous evening; as to bathing, none of them were likely to go and indulge in such a luxury.

To Cold-Water Spring we went; but they were not to be

seen, nor could the other men give any account of them.

The lieutenant burst into a fit of laughter, not unmixed with vexation.

"A pretty set of troops I have to command—my sergeant sick, one drunk, and two missing."

"Probably Klitz and Gillooly have only taken a ramble, and will soon be back," I observed; "and by that time the other fellow will have recovered from his tipsy fit; so it is of no use to be vexed. You should be more anxious about Sergeant Custis, for I fear he will not be able to accompany you for several days to come."

On going back to the house, we found the sergeant no better. Rachel, indeed, said that he was in a raging fever, and that he must have suffered from a sunstroke, or something of that sort.

The lieutenant was now almost in despair; and though the dispatches he carried were not of vital importance, yet they ought, he said, to be delivered as soon as possible, and he had already delayed two days. As there was no help for it, however, and he could not at all events set out until his men came back, I invited him to take a fishing-rod and accompany me to a part of the stream where, although he might not catch many fish, he would at all events enjoy the scenery.

It was a wild place; the rocks rose to a sheer height of two or three hundred feet above our heads, broken into a variety of fantastic forms. In one place there was a cleft in the rock, out of which the water flowed into the main stream. The lieutenant, who was fond of fishing, was soon absorbed in the sport, and, as I expected, forgot his troubles about his men.

He had caught several trout and a couple of catfish, when I saw Rachel hurrying towards us.

"Massa Sergeant much worse," she exclaimed; "him fear him die; want bery much to see him officer, so I come away while Missie Clarice watch ober him. Him bery quiet now,—no fear ob him crying out for present."

On hearing this, we gathered up our fishing-rods and hastened back to the house, considerably outwalking Rachel, who came puffing after us.

We found Clarice standing by the bedside of the sick man, moistening his parched lips, and driving away the flies from his face.

"I am afraid I am going, sir," he said as the lieutenant bent over him. "Before I die, I wish to tell you that I do not trust those two men of ours, Karl Klitz and Gillooly. I learned from Pat Sperry that they have been constantly putting their heads together of late, and he suspects that they intend either to desert, or to do some mischief or other."

"Thank you," said the lieutenant; "but do not trouble yourself about such matters now. I will look after the men. You must try to keep your mind quiet. I hope that you are not going to die, as you suppose. I have seen many men look much worse than you do, and yet recover."

The sergeant, after he had relieved his mind, appeared to be more quiet. Rachel insisted on his taking some of her remedies; and as evening drew on he was apparently better,—at all events, no worse. Clarice and the negress were unremitting in their attentions, utterly regardless of the fever being infectious; I do not think, indeed, that the idea that it was so ever entered their heads.

The lieutenant had been so occupied with his poor sergeant, that he seemed to have forgotten all about his missing men. At last, however, he recollected them, and I went back with him to the hut.

On the way we looked into the stables, where we found the five horses and baggage-mules all right; so that the men, if they had deserted, must have done so on foot.

We opened the door of the hut, hoping that possibly by this time the missing men might have returned; but neither of them was there. The drunken fellow was, however, still sleeping on, and probably would have slept on until his hut companions came back, had we not roused him up.

"You must take care that your people do not give him any more liquor, or he will be in the same state to-morrow morning," observed the lieutenant.

We had some difficulty in bringing the man to his senses; but the lieutenant finding a pitcher of water, poured the contents over him, which effectually roused him up.

"Hullo! murther! are we all going to be drowned entirely at the bottom? Sure the river's burst over us!" he exclaimed, springing out of his bunk. He looked very much astonished at seeing the lieutenant and me; but quickly bringing himself into position, and giving a military salute, "All right, your honour," said he.

"Yes, I see that you are so now," said the lieutenant; "but little help you could have afforded us, had we been attacked by the enemy. I must call you to account by-and-by. What has become of your comrades?"

"Sure, your honour, are they not all sleeping sweetly as

infants in their bunks?" He peered as he spoke into the bunks which had been occupied by the other men. "The drunken bastes, it was there I left them barely two hours ago, while I jist turned in to get a quiet snooze. They are not there now, your honour," he observed, with a twinkle in his eye; "they must have gone out unbeknown to me. It is mighty surprising!"

"Why, you impudent rascal, you have been asleep for the last twelve hours," said the lieutenant, scarcely able to restrain his gravity. "Take care that this does not happen again; keep sober while you remain here."

"Sure, your honour, I would not touch a dhrop of the cratur, even if they were to try and pour it down me throat," he answered. "But I found a countryman of mine living here. It is a hard matter, when one meets a boy from Old Ireland, to refuse jist a sip of the potheen for the sake of gintility!"

"Follow me to the house as soon as you have put yourself into decent order," said the lieutenant, not wishing to exchange further words with the trooper.

Pat touched his hat, to signify that he would obey the order, and the lieutenant and I walked on.

"I cannot put that fellow under arrest, seeing that I have no one to whom I can give him in charge," said the lieutenant, laughing. "But what can have become of the others? I do not think, notwithstanding what Sergeant Custis said, that they can have deserted. They would scarcely make an attempt to get over this wild country alone, and on foot."

As soon as Pat made his appearance, the lieutenant ordered him to stand on guard at the door, where he kept him until nightfall.

When our men came in, I inquired whether they knew anything of the troopers. They one and all averred that they had left them sleeping in the hut, and that they had no notion where they could have gone.

"Could the fellows, when probably as drunk as Pat, have fallen into the torrent and been drowned!" exclaimed the lieutenant anxiously.

"Sure, they were as sober as judges," observed Dan, one of our men. Then an idea seemed to strike him. "To be sure, your honour, they might have gone fishing up the stream. That broth of a boy Barney might jist have rolled in, and the long Dutchman have tried to haul him out, and both have been carried away together. Ill luck to Roaring Water, if it has swallowed up my countryman Barney."

I suspected, from the way in which Dan spoke, that he had no great belief that such a catastrophe had occurred; in fact, knowing the fellow pretty well, I thought it very probable that, notwithstanding what he said, he was cognisant of the whereabouts of the truants.

Uncle Jeff and the lieutenant examined and cross-examined all the men; but no satisfactory information could be got out of them.

"Whether they come back or not, I must be on my way to-morrow morning with Sperry; while I leave my sergeant under your care, if you will take charge of him," said the lieutenant.

Uncle Jeff willingly undertook to do this.

"As you are unacquainted with the way, and Pat is not likely to be of much assistance, if Uncle Jeff will allow me I will act as your guide to the mouth of the pass, after which you will have no great difficulty in finding your way to Fort Harwood," I said to the lieutenant.

He gladly accepted my offer.

"But what about the possibility of the farm being attacked by the Indians? You would not like in that case to be absent, and I should be unwilling to deprive your friends of your aid," he observed. "If you accompany me, I must leave Sperry to attend on Sergeant Custis, and to come on with him when he is well enough. Although I do not compare the Irishman to you, yet, should the farm be attacked, I can answer for his firing away as long as he has a bullet left in his pouch."

Uncle Jeff, much to my satisfaction, allowed me to accompany the lieutenant. I had a good horse, too, and had no fears about making my way back safely, even should the country be swarming with Indians.

When the lieutenant spoke of the possibility of the farm being attacked by the Redskins, Uncle Jeff laughed. "They will not venture thus far," he observed. "But even if they do come, we will give a good account of them. Not to speak of my rifle, Bartle's and Gideon's are each worth fifty muskets in the hands of the Indians; our other four fellows, with your trooper, will keep the rest at bay, however many there may be of them. The sergeant, too, will be able to handle a rifle before long, I hope; while Clarice and Rachel will load the arms, and look after any of us who may be hurt. But we need not talk about that; the varmints will not trouble us, you may depend upon it."

When Bartle Won heard of the disappearance of the troopers, and that we had examined our men, but had been unable to elicit any information from them as to what had become of the truants, he observed,—"Leave that to me. If they know anything about the matter, I will get it out of them before long. As to the fellows having tumbled into the torrent, I do not believe it. They are not likely to have gone off without our people knowing something about it. They are either in hiding somewhere near Roaring Water,—and if so, I shall soon ferret them out,—or else they have gone away to take squaws from among the Indians, and set up for themselves."

The lieutenant did not think that the latter proceeding was very probable; but their absence was mysterious, and we had to confess that we were no wiser as to their whereabouts than we were at first.

CHAPTER THREE

MY FAMILY HISTORY—MY FATHER, ONCE A CAPTAIN IN THE BRITISH ARMY, COMES TO AMERICA AND MARRIES UNCLE JEFF'S SISTER—HE SETTLES ON A FARM IN OHIO—CLARICE AND I ARE BORN—MY GRANDFATHER'S FARM DESTROYED BY A FLOOD—THE NEXT YEAR OUR FARM IS BURNT—MY FATHER RESOLVES TO MIGRATE TO THE WEST—WE SET OFF IN WAGGONS WITH AN EMIGRANT TRAIN—PROSPEROUS COMMENCEMENT OF JOURNEY—PROVISIONS RUN SHORT—I WITNESS A BUFFALO HUNT—THE EMIGRANTS SUFFER FROM CHOLERA—MY MOTHER DIES—MANY OF THE EMIGRANTS TURN BACK—MY FATHER PERSEVERES—FIERCELY ATTACKED BY INDIANS—WE KEEP THEM AT BAY—AGAIN ATTACKED, WHEN A STRANGER COMES TO OUR ASSISTANCE—CLARICE GIVES HIM A BOOK—HE PROMISES TO READ IT—WE CONTINUE OUR JOURNEY, AND REACH FORT KEARNEY—REMAIN THERE FOR SOME MONTHS—MY FATHER, THOUGH STILL SUFFERING, INSISTS ON SETTING OUT AGAIN—HE SOON BECOMES WORSE, AND DIES—I AM DIGGING HIS GRAVE, WHEN AN EMIGRANT TRAIN COMES BY—UNCLE JEFF IS THE LEADER, AND WE ACCOMPANY HIM TO ROARING WATER

But the readers of my Journal, if so I may venture to call it, would like to know how Clarice and I came to be at Uncle Jeff's farm. To do so, I must give a little bit of my family history, which probably would not otherwise interest them.

My father, Captain Middlemore, had been an officer in the English army, but sold out and came to America. Being, I suspect, of a roving disposition, he had travelled through most of the Eastern States without finding any spot where he could make up his mind to settle. At length he bent his steps to Ohio; in the western part of which he had one night to seek shelter from a storm at the farm of a substantial settler, a Mr Ralph Crockett (the father of Uncle Jeff). Mr Crockett treated the English stranger with a hospitality which the farmers of Ohio never failed to show to their guests. He had several sons, but he spoke of one who seemed to have a warm place in his heart, and who had gone away some years before, and was leading a wild hunter's life on the prairies.

"I should like to fall in with him," said my father. "It is the sort of life I have a fancy for leading,—hunting the buffalo and fighting the Red Indian."

"Better stay and settle down among us, stranger," said Mr Crockett. "In a few years, if you turn to with a will, and have some little money to begin with, you will be a wealthy man, with broad acres of your own, and able to supply the Eastern States with thousands of bushels of wheat. It is a proud thing to feel that we feed, not only the people of our own land, but many who would be starving, if it were not for us, in that tax-burdened country of yours."

My father laughed at the way in which the Ohio farmer spoke of Old England; but notwithstanding that, he thought the matter over seriously. He was influenced not a little, too, I have an idea, by the admiration he felt for the farmer's only daughter, Mary Crockett.

My father had the price of his commission still almost intact; and it was looked upon as almost a princely fortune to begin with in that part of the world. So, as he received no hint to go,—indeed, he was warmly pressed to stay whenever he spoke of moving,—he stayed, and stayed on. At last he asked Mary Crockett to become his wife, and promised to settle down on the nearest farm her father could obtain for him.

Mr Crockett applauded his resolution; and he purchased a farm which happened to be for sale only a few miles off, and gave him his daughter for a wife. She had gone to school in Philadelphia, where she had gained sufficient accomplishments to satisfy my father's fastidious taste; and she was, besides being very pretty, a Christian young woman.

She often spoke of her brother Jeff with warm affection, for he, when at home, had ever showed himself to be a loving, kind brother; indeed, Mary was his pet, and if anybody could have induced him to lead a settled life, she might have done it. He had had, somehow or other, a quarrel with her one day,—little more than a tiff,—so off he went into the woods and across the prairies; and, as it turned out, he never came back. She was not the cause of his going, for he had been thinking about it for a long time before, but this tiff just set the ball rolling.

My parents were perfectly happy in their married life, and might have remained so had it not been for my poor father's unsettled disposition. I was born, then Clarice; and both my father and mother devoted all the time they could spare from the duties of the farm to our education. Clarice was always a bright, intelligent little creature, and rapidly took in all the instruction she received. My mother's only unhappiness arose from the thought of sending her to Philadelphia,—

where she might have to complete her education, as she wished her to become as perfect a lady as our father was a thorough gentleman. He, being well informed, was able to instruct me, and I made as much progress as my sister. Rough in some respects as were our lives, we found the advantage of this, as we could enjoy many amusements from which we should otherwise have been debarred. Clarice learned to play and sing from our mother; and I was especially fond of drawing, an art in which my father was well able to instruct me.

But our family, hitherto prosperous, were now to suffer severe reverses. My grandfather's property lay in a rich bottom, and one early spring the floods came and swept away his corn-fields, destroyed his meadows, and carried off his cattle. One of my uncles was drowned at that time, another died of fever caught from exposure, and a third was killed by the fall of a tree. The old man did not complain at God's dealing with him, for he was a true Christian, but he bowed his head; and he died shortly afterwards, at our house. My father's property had escaped the floods, but the following summer, which was an unusually dry one, a fire swept over the country. It reached our farm, and although my father had timely notice, so that he was able to put my mother and us into one of the waggons, with the most valuable part of his household property, the rest was enveloped in flames shortly after we had left the house. The next day not a building, not a fence, remained standing. The whole farm was a scene of black desolation.

"We have had a pretty strong hint to move westward, which I have long been thinking of doing," said my father. "Many who have gone to the Pacific coast have become possessed of wealth in half the time we have taken to get this farm in order. What do you say, Mary?"

Our mother was always ready to do whatever he wished, although she would rather have remained in the part of the country where she was born and still had many friends.

"I should say, let us go eastward, and purchase a small farm in some more civilised district; we can then send our children to school, and be able to see them during the holidays," she observed.

"We ourselves can give them such schooling as they require," replied my father. "You will make Clarice as accomplished as yourself, and I will take good care of Ralph. It is not book learning a lad requires to get on in this country. He is a good hand at shooting and fishing, understands all sorts of farm work, and is as good a rider as any boy of his age. He will forget all these accomplishments if we go eastward; whereas if we move westward, he will improve still more. And as he is as sharp as a Yankee, he will do well enough in whatever line he follows."

The truth was, my father had made up his mind to go in the direction he proposed, and was not to be turned aside by any arguments, however sensible, which my mother might offer. So it was settled that we should make a long journey across the prairie. As for the difficulties and dangers to be encountered, or the hardships to which my mother and Clarice would be exposed, he did not take these into consideration. There are people with minds so constituted that they only see one side of a question; and my father was unhappily one of these.

He proposed to unite himself with some respectable party of emigrants, who would travel together for mutual protection. He considered that they might thus set at defiance any band of Indians, however numerous, which they might encounter.

The two farms were no doubt much inferior in value to what they would have been with buildings, outhouses and fencings, standing crops and stock; yet, even as they stood, they were worth a good sum, for they were already cleared—the chief work of the settler being thus done. However, they realised as much as my father expected, and with a well-equipped train and several hired attendants we set out.

The first part of our journey was tolerably easy; the emigrants were good-humoured, we had abundance of provisions, the country was well watered, and the cattle could obtain plenty of rich grass to keep up their strength. But as soon as we got out of the more civilised districts our difficulties began. Some of the rivers were very difficult to cross, and often there was no small danger of the waggons sticking fast in some spots, or being carried down by the current in others; then we had hills to surmount and rocky ground to pass over, where there was no herbage or water for our beasts.

My father kept aloof as much as possible from the other emigrants, so that we did not hear of the complaints they were making. At last a rumour reached us that the owners of several of the waggons were talking of turning back. We had met at different times two or three trains of people who had given up the journey, and these had declared that the hardships were greater than any human beings could bear; but my father had made up his mind, and go on he would, even if he carried his own waggons alone over the prairie. A few Indians hovered round us at times, but our rifle-shots warned them to keep off; and at night we encamped, under my father's direction, in military fashion, with the waggons placed so as to form a fortification round the camp.

Our fresh provisions had come to an end, too, and it now became very important that we should procure game.

We had encamped one evening, when several Indians approached, making signs that they were friends. They proved to belong to a tribe which had been at peace with the white people. Our guide knew one of them, and we had no doubt that they could be trusted. They have long since been driven from their old hunting-grounds, and I forget even the name of the tribe. When they heard that we were in want of fresh food, they said that if any of our hunters would accompany them they would show us where buffalo could be found; and that we might either shoot them ourselves, or that they would try to kill some for us.

Few of our people, although hardy backwoodsmen, were accustomed to hunting; and few, indeed, had ever seen any buffalo. But my father, feeling the importance of obtaining some fresh meat, volunteered to go,—directing a light cart to follow, in order to bring back our game,—and I obtained leave to accompany him.

One of the Indians could speak English sufficiently well to make himself understood by us. Talking to my father, and finding that even he had never shot any buffalo, the Indian advised that we should allow him and his people to attack the herd in their own manner, as the animals might take alarm before we could get up to them, and escape us altogether. My father agreed to this, saying that, should they fail, he would be ready with his rifle to ride after the herd and try to bring down one or more of them. This plan was agreed to, and we rode forward.

I observed our Indian friend dismount and put his ear to the ground several times as we rode forward. My father asked him why he did this. He replied that it was to ascertain how far off the buffalo were: he could judge of the distance by the sound of their feet, and their occasional roars as the bulls engaged in combat. Not an animal, however, was yet visible.

At last we caught sight of a number of dark objects moving on the prairie in the far distance.

"There is the herd!" exclaimed the Indian; "we must now be wary how we approach."

Still we went on, the animals being too busily engaged in grazing, or in attacking each other, to observe us. At last the Indian advised that we should halt behind a knoll which rose out of the plain, with a few bushes on the summit. Here we could remain concealed from the herd. So, having gained the foot of the knoll, we dismounted; and leaving our horses in charge of the men with the cart, my father and I climbed up to the top, where by crouching down we were unseen by the herd, although we could observe all that was going forward.

The Indian hunters now took some wolf-skins which had been hanging to their saddles, and completely covering themselves up, so as to represent wolves, they began to creep towards the herd, trailing their rifles at their sides; thus they got nearer and nearer the herd. Whenever any of the animals stopped to look at them, they stopped also; when the buffalo went on feeding, they advanced. At length each hunter, having selected a cow, suddenly sprang to his knees and fired, and three fine animals rolled over; though, had the buffalo bulls known their power, they might, with the greatest ease, have crushed their human foes. On hearing the shots, the whole herd took to flight.

"Well done!" cried my father. "I should like to have another, though;" and hurrying down the hill, he mounted his horse and galloped off in chase of the retreating herd.

Heavy and clumsy as the animals looked, so rapidly did they rush over the ground that he could only got within range of two or three of the rearmost. Pulling up, he fired; but the buffalo dashed on; and, unwilling to fatigue his horse, my father came back, somewhat annoyed at his failure.

The three animals which had been killed were quickly cut up, and we loaded our cart with the meat; after which the Indians accompanied us back to the camp to receive the reward we had promised. The supply of fresh meat was very welcome, and helped to keep sickness at a distance for some time longer.

After this we made several days' journey, the supply of fresh provisions putting all hands into better spirits than they had shown for some time. There was but little chance, however, of our replenishing our stock when that was exhausted, for we saw Indians frequently hovering round our camp who were not likely to prove as friendly as those we had before met with, and it would be dangerous to go to any distance in search of game, as there was a probability of our being cut off by them.

We had soon another enemy to contend with, more subtile than even the Redskins. Cholera broke out among the emigrants, and one after another succumbed. This determined those who had before talked of going back to carry out their intentions; and notwithstanding the expostulations of my father and others, they turned round the heads of their cattle, and back they went over the road we had come.

I had by this time observed that my mother was not looking so well as usual. One night she became very ill, and in spite of all my father and two kind women of our party could do for her, before morning she was dead. My father appeared inconsolable; and, naturally, Clarice and I were very unhappy. We would willingly have died with her.

"But we must not complain at what God ordains," said

Clarice; "we must wish to live, to be of use to poor papa. She is happy, we know; she trusted in Christ, and has gone to dwell with him."

Clarice succeeded better than I did in soothing our poor father's grief. I thought that he himself would now wish to go back, but he was too proud to think of doing that. He had become the acknowledged leader of the party, and the sturdy men who remained with us were now all for going forward; so, after we had buried our dear mother in a grove of trees which grew near the camp, and had built a monument of rough stones over her grave, to mark the spot, we once more moved forward.

We had just formed our camp the next day, in a more exposed situation than usual, when we saw a party of mounted Indians hovering in the distance. My father, who had not lifted his head until now, gave orders for the disposal of the waggons as could best be done. There were not sufficient to form a large circle, however, so that our fortifications were less strong than they had before been. We made the cattle graze as close to the camp as possible, so that they might be driven inside at a moment's notice; and of course we kept strict watch, one half of the men only lying down at a time.

The night had almost passed away without our being assailed, when just before dawn those on watch shouted out—

"Here they are! Up, up, boys! got in the cattle—quick!"

Just as the last animal was driven inside our fortifications the enemy were upon us. We received them with a hot fire, which emptied three saddles; when, according to their fashion, they lifted up their dead or wounded companions and carried them off out of the range of our rifles.

Our men shouted, thinking that they had gained the victory; but the Indians were only preparing for another assault. Seeing the smallness of our numbers, they were persuaded that they could overwhelm us; and soon we caught sight of them moving round so as to encircle our camp, and thus attack us on all sides at once.

"Remember the women and children," cried my father, whose spirit was now aroused. "If we give in, we and they will be massacred; so we can do nothing but fight to the last."

The men shouted, and vowed to stand by each other.

Before the Indians, however, got within range of our rifles, they wheeled round and galloped off again, but we could still see them hovering round us. It was pretty evident that they had not given up the intention of attacking us; their object being to weary us out, and make our hearts, as they would call it, turn pale.

Just before the sun rose above the horizon they once more came on, decreasing the circumference of the circle, and gradually closing in upon us; not at a rapid rate, however, but slowly—sometimes so slowly that they scarcely appeared to move.

"Do not fire, friends, until you can take good aim," cried my father, as the enemy got within distant rifle range. "It is just what they wish us to do; then they will come charging down upon us, in the hope of finding our rifles unloaded. Better let them come sufficiently near to see their eyes; alternate men of you only fire."

The savages were armed only with bows and spears; still they could shoot their arrows, we knew, when galloping at full speed.

At a sign from one of their leaders they suddenly put their horses to full speed, at the same time giving vent to what I can only describe as a mingling of shrieks and shouts and howls, forming the terrific Indian war-whoop. They were mistaken, however, if they expected to frighten our sturdy backwoodsmen. The first of our men fired when they were about twenty yards off. Several of the red warriors were knocked over, but the rest came on, shooting their arrows, and fancying that they had to attack men with empty firearms. The second shots were full in their faces, telling therefore with great effect; while our people raised a shout, which, if not as shrill, was almost as telling as that of the Indian war-whoop. The first men who had fired were ramming away with all their might to reload, and were able to deliver a second fire; while those who had pistols discharged them directly afterwards.

The Indians, supposing that our party, although we had but few waggons, must be far more numerous than they had expected, wheeled round without attempting to break through the barricade, and galloped off at full speed,—not even attempting to pick up those who had fallen.

The women and children, with Clarice, I should have said, had been protected by a barricade of bales and chests; so that, although a number of arrows had flown into our enclosure, not one of them was hurt.

On looking at my father, I saw that he was paler than usual; and what was my dismay to find that an arrow had entered his side! It was quickly cut out, although the operation caused him much suffering. He declared, however, that it was only a flesh wound, and not worth taking into consideration.

The Indians being still near us, we thought it only too probable that we should again be attacked. And, indeed, our anticipations were soon fully realised. In less than half an hour, after having apparently been reinforced, they once more came on, but this time with; the intention of attacking only one side.

We were looking about us, however, in every direction, to ascertain what manoeuvres they might adopt, when we saw to the westward another body of horsemen coming across the prairie.

"We are to have a fresh band of them upon us," cried some of our party.

"No, no," I shouted out; "they are white men! I see their rifle-barrels glancing in the sun; and there are no plumes above their heads!"

I was right; and before many minutes were over the Indians had seen them too, and, not liking their looks, had galloped off to the southward.

We received the strangers with cheers as they drew near; and they proved to be a large body of traders.

"We heard your shots, and guessed that those Pawnee rascals were upon you," said their leader, as he dismounted.

He came up to where my father was lying by the side of the waggon.

"I am sorry to see that you are hurt, friend," he said. "Any of the rest of your people wounded? If there are, and your party will come on to our camp, we will render you all the assistance in our power."

"Only two of our men have been hit, and that but slightly; and my wound is nothing," answered my father. "We are much obliged to you, however."

"Well, at all events I would advise you to harness your beasts and move on, or these fellows will be coming back again," said the stranger. "We too must not stay here long, for if they think that our camp is left unguarded they may pay it a visit." His eye, as he was speaking, fell on Clarice. "Why! my little maiden, were you not frightened at seeing those fierce horsemen galloping up to your camp?" he asked.

"No," she answered simply; "I trusted in God, for I knew that he would take care of us."

The stranger gazed at her with surprise, and said something which made her look up.

"Why! don't you always trust in God?" she asked.

"I don't think much about him; and I don't suppose he thinks much about such a wild fellow as I am," he said in a careless tone.

"I wish you would, then," she said; "nobody can be happy if they do not trust in God and accept his offer of salvation, because they cannot feel secure for a moment without his love and protection; and they will not know where they are to go to when they die."

"I have not thought about that," said the stranger, in the same tone as before; "and I do not suppose I am likely to find it out."

"Then let me give you a book," said Clarice, "which will tell you all about it."

She went to the waggon, and brought out a small Bible.

"There! If you will read that, and do what it tells, you will become wise and happy."

"Well, my dear, I will accept your book, and do as you advise me. I once knew something about the Bible, before I left home, years and years ago; but I have not looked into one since."

Without opening the book, the stranger placed it in his breast-pocket; then, after exchanging a few words with my father, who promised to follow his advice, he left the camp and rejoined his companions.

My father, being unable to ride without difficulty, had himself placed in the waggon by the side of Clarice; and the animals being put to, we once more moved on to the westward, while we saw our late visitors take an easterly course.

My father, however, made but slow progress towards recovery; his wound was more serious than he had supposed, and it was too clear that he was in a very unfit state to undergo the fatigue of a journey.

We at length reached Fort Kearney, on the Platte River, where we met with a kind reception from the officers of the garrison, while my father received that attention from the surgeon he so much required. The rest of our party were unwilling to delay longer than was necessary; but the surgeon assured my father that he would risk his life should he continue, in the state in which he then was, to prosecute his journey. Very unwillingly, therefore, he consented to remain,—for our sakes more than his own,—while our late companions proceeded towards their destination. We here remained several months, of course at great expense, as both our men and animals had to be fed, although we ourselves were entertained without cost by our hospitable hosts.

At last another emigrant train halted at the post, and my father, unwilling longer to trespass on the kindness of his entertainers, insisted on continuing his journey with them. The surgeon warned him that he would do so at great risk; observing that should the wound, which was scarcely healed, break out again, it would prove a serious matter. Still, his desire to be actively engaged in forming the new settlement prevailed over all other considerations, and on a fatal day he started, in company with about a dozen other waggons. The owners, who were rough farmers, took very little interest either in my poor father or in us.

We had been travelling for about ten days or a fortnight when my father again fell ill. He tried to proceed in the waggon, but was unable to bear the jolting; and we were at length obliged to remain in camp by ourselves, while the rest of the train continued on the road. Our camp was pitched in an angle formed by a broad stream on the side of a wood, so that we were pretty well protected should enemies on horseback attack us. My father proposed to remain here to await another emigrant train, hoping in a short time to be sufficiently recovered to move on. But, to our great grief, Clarice and I saw that he was rapidly sinking. He himself did not appear to be aware of his condition; and fearing that it would aggravate his sufferings were he to think he was about to leave us, young as we were, in the midst of the wild prairie among strangers, we were unwilling to tell him what we thought.

The men with us began to grumble at the long delay, and declared their intention of moving forward with the next emigrant train which should come by. But what was our dismay, one morning, to find that both the villains had gone, carrying off the cart, and a considerable amount of our property! We were not aware at this time, however, that they had managed to get hold of the chest which contained our money. Our father was so ill, too, that we did not tell him what had occurred; and that very evening, as Clarice and I were sitting by his side holding his hands, he ceased to breathe.

At first we could not persuade ourselves that he was dead. That was indeed a terrible night. I felt, however, that something must be done, and that the first thing was to bury our poor father. We had spades and pick-axes in the waggon, so, taking one of each, I commenced my melancholy task near the banks of a stream.

I was thus engaged when I heard Clarice cry out; and on looking up I saw a small emigrant train passing, which must have been encamped at no great distance from us down the river. Fearing that they might pass without observing us, I ran forward shouting out, entreating the leader to stop. The train immediately came to a standstill, and a man advanced towards me, in whom I soon recognised the person to whom Clarice had given the book many months before.

"Why, my man," he said, "I thought I knew you! How are your sister and your father? He had got an ugly hurt, I recollect, when I saw him."

"He is just dead," I answered.

"Dead!" he exclaimed; "and are you two young ones left on the prairie alone?"

"Yes," I replied; "our men have made off, and I was going to beg you to take us along with you."

"That I will do right gladly," said the stranger.

When I told him how I was engaged, he immediately sent some of his men, and they at once set to work and dug a deep grave. Our poor father having then been placed in it, they raised over it a pile of heavy logs.

"I wish we could have done better for him," said the stranger; "but many a fine fellow sleeps under such a monument as that."

I need not dwell upon our grief as we watched these proceedings. I was sure that the sooner Clarice was away from the spot the better it would be for her; so, as the leader of the emigrant train did not wish to delay longer than was necessary, I assisted in harnessing the animals to our waggon, and we at once moved on.

I was walking beside our new friend, when he asked me my name.

"Ralph Middlemore," I replied; "and my sister is called Clarice."

"Ralph!" repeated the stranger; "that was my father's name."

"I was called after my grandfather," I observed,—"Ralph Crockett."

I do not know how I came to say that. My companion

started, and gazing at me attentively, asked,—"What was your mother's name?"

"Mary."

"Where is she now?" he inquired eagerly.

"She died after we began this sad journey," I said.

The stranger was silent, stifling some deep emotion.

"Your sister is like her,—very like what she was at the same age. You have heard of Jeff Crockett, boy? I am your Uncle Jeff; and though I have much to mourn for, I thank Heaven I was sent to rescue Mary's children in their distress. And Clarice! she has been to me as an angel of light. You remember that she gave me a book. I took it to please her, not intending to read it; but I did read it, and it showed me what I was—a wretched, lost sinner. I learned that I was like the prodigal son; and as I heard that my earthly father was no more, I determined to go to my Heavenly Father, knowing that he would receive me. He has done so, and I can now say honestly that I am a Christian, and fit to take charge of Mary's children."

I need say very little more than that from this time Uncle Jeff constituted himself our guardian, and that we thankfully accompanied him to the new location he was forming at Roaring Water.

And now I shall resume my narrative at the point at which I interrupted it to give the reader a bit of my family history.

CHAPTER FOUR

AS THE LIEUTENANT AND I ARE STARTING, WE HEAR THAT KLITZ AND BARNEY HAVE GONE OFF WITH A WHEEL-BARROW FOR CALIFORNIA—A PLEASANT BIVOUAC—AT LAST WE CATCH SIGHT OF THE DESERTERS—THE LIEUTENANT IS ABOUT TO RIDE AFTER THEM, WHEN A PARTY OF INDIANS APPEAR—THE INDIANS TAKE TO FLIGHT, AND WE LOSE SIGHT OF THE RUNAWAYS—FORM OUR CAMP—DISCOVER THAT WE ARE WATCHED—FOLLOW THE SPY, WHO PROVES TO BE MAYSOTTA—FIND THE DESERTERS TAKING THEIR EASE—WE CAPTURE THEM, AND, GUIDED BY MAYSOTTA, TAKE THEM TO THE INDIAN CAMP—RESOLVE TO RETURN TO THE FARM.

The lieutenant and I had arranged to start at daybreak, on horseback, with a couple of baggage-mules carrying provisions and camp utensils. Clarice was up to give us our breakfast, and I heard the lieutenant tell her how much he hoped to meet her again.

"Not very likely, in this wild region," she answered with perfect composure, although a slight blush came to her cheek as she spoke.

The lieutenant having given directions to Pat to remain and do his duty,—charging him not to get drunk again, and to come on with the sergeant as soon as he was able to travel,—we were on the point of mounting our horses, when Bartle came up.

"I thought that I should get something out of our fellows," he said. "Of all the strange things I have ever heard of people doing, the strangest is what your two troopers are attempting. It seems that the Dutchman and the Irish chap have taken possession of one of our wheelbarrows and a couple of pick-axes and spades, with such other things as they had a fancy for, and have gone off, expecting to make their way to California, where, it is said, gold can be had to any amount by digging for it."

"The rascals!" exclaimed the lieutenant; "they will not get there in a hurry, and we shall probably come up with them before long."

"They have had a good many days' start of you," observed Bartle, "and if they have kept on going, they must be some distance on their road by this time."

"Then we must push on all the faster," said the lieutenant. "I should like to catch the fellows before the Indians take their scalps; although, when we have got them, it will be difficult to know what to do with them, as they will delay me while they move slowly along on foot."

"Send them back to us; we will soon show them how to use their picks and spades," said Bartle.

After the usual hand-shaking at parting, and the lieutenant had once more lifted his cap to Clarice, who stood at the door watching us, we set off down the hill, each of us leading a baggage-mule by the bridle.

Every inch of the way, for some miles, was known to me, so that we could move on without troubling ourselves about the road. We had occasionally hills to go over, spurs of the big mountains on our left; but we kept as much we could on the level ground,—sometimes having to make a detour for the sake of avoiding the rocky heights, which were inaccessible to our animals.

As the day advanced we began to look out for the runaways, although the lieutenant was of opinion that they must be still some way ahead of us. We also kept our eyes open on the chance of any Indians coming down upon us,—although I did not think that there was much risk of that; for every one at the farm had been convinced that the Arrapahas had long since gone away to the southward, and that we should hear no more of them.

That night we encamped at a snug spot near a stream, with a wood to the southward almost surrounding us, so that the light of our fire could not be seen by any one on that side. There was rich grass for our animals, and they were therefore not likely to stray. We were both young, in good health and spirits, and with no cares to oppress us, so we greatly enjoyed our bivouac. We sat by the fire chatting away for some time; then we lay down, wrapped in our buffalo robes, to sleep, resolving to awake at intervals, in order to put on fresh fuel, as it was important not to let our fire get low. Fortunately, we awoke as often as was needful, and by maintaining a good blaze we kept at a distance any bears or wolves which might have been prowling about. The next morning, at daybreak, we once more moved on. As yet, we had discovered no signs of the runaways; indeed, when we came to think over the matter, we considered that they would probably have kept out of the beaten track, in order to avoid discovery should they be pursued. From the nature of the ground, they would not have gone to the left; and I therefore suggested that we should keep to the right, where, if they really were making for the pass, we should be pretty certain of coming upon them. We accordingly struck off at an angle in the direction I proposed, and then once more continued our former course northward, keeping a bright look-out ahead and on either side.

"If the fellows are still before us, they deserve credit for the speed at which they must have been travelling," observed the lieutenant.

"But, notwithstanding, we shall be up with them before dark," I exclaimed. "See there!" and I pointed to a mark on the grass, which my quick eye had detected as that made by a single wheel.

The lieutenant, however, could not see it, and thought that my fancy was deceiving me.

Had we not been detained by the baggage-mules, we should, I was sure, have quickly overtaken the runaways. I must own, however, that I felt very little interest in their capture, for I considered them not worth their salt as soldiers,—a couple of "Uncle Sam's" hard bargains,—but the lieutenant had no wish to be blamed for losing his men, should he arrive at the fort without his escort.

We had to call a halt twice in the day, to allow our animals to feed and drink, and to take some refreshment ourselves. Two or three times, as I looked round, I fancied that I saw some objects in the distance; it might have been Indians or deer, or perhaps even buffalo, although the latter seldom came so close to the mountains.

We, of course, kept our arms ready for any emergency; and as but few of the natives in those regions had at that time firearms, I knew that Indians would be very wary how they approached within range of our rifles.

The day was drawing to a close, and I was looking out for a convenient spot for camping, when I saw in the far distance ahead of us, and just on the summit of some rising ground, a couple of figures.

"Who can these be?" exclaimed the lieutenant, who saw them at the same time.

"Unless I am greatly mistaken, they are your two deserters, Klitz and Gillooly."

We dragged on the unwilling mules, in the endeavour to overtake them; but I think the fellows must have seen us, for they moved forward at a rapid rate. The fat little Irishman was ahead trundling the wheel-barrow, while the tall German followed close at his heels carrying a couple of muskets, one over each shoulder.

"Stay by the mules, Ralph; pray do!" exclaimed the lieutenant. "I will gallop after the rascals, and bring them to a halt."

"There is a deep stream between us and them," I observed, "and you may have some difficulty in crossing it alone; we will follow at our leisure, for we are sure to catch them up before dark."

Just as I spoke, the ominous cry of an Indian war-whoop came from behind us; and looking round, we saw nearly a dozen mounted warriors coming on at full gallop. To throw ourselves from our horses, and to get our rifles ready for firing, was the work of a moment.

The Indians had expected to see us take to flight, so on observing our determined attitude they pulled rein. They stopped and watched us for some time; and then, apparently considering that the risk they would run of certainly losing two of their number, if not more, was not worth the object to be attained, they wheeled round and galloped off in the direction from whence they had come.

We continued watching them until they had disappeared in the distance; and when we turned about and again looked for the runaways, they were nowhere to be seen.

"Never fear," I observed; "we shall soon catch them up. But I would rather that those Redskin fellows, if they are enemies, had not been in the neighbourhood; for they may take it into their heads to pay us a visit while we are encamped at night. Knowing, however, that we are well armed, and likely to be prepared for them, they will not attack us openly; yet they will, if they can, steal up to our camp, and try to take us by surprise."

Our great object now was to find a secure camping-ground; so we pushed on, and I led my companion across the stream by a ford somewhat further up. But still we saw nothing of Klitz or Gillooly, while the waning light prevented me from discovering their trail, had they crossed where we did. Some way ahead was a large wood, which extended to the very foot of the mountains, and within its recesses we should be able to shelter ourselves from any onset of horsemen, although the trees would favour the approach of enemies who might attempt to take us by surprise.

We rode on, skirting the forest as long as we had sufficient light to distinguish objects at any distance, still with the hope that we might find the runaways encamped, in case they should not have seen us. That they had not perceived us, near as we were to them, was quite possible, as their backs had been turned towards us the whole time they were in sight; and their moving on so quickly might be accounted for by their wish to reach a good spot for camping on before dark.

We ourselves, after searching about for some time, and being unable to find any traces of them, resolved to encamp in a small recess in the wood which presented itself. There was water near, from a rivulet which came winding through the forest, and plenty of grass. We accordingly hobbled and staked our horses close at hand; and we then collected wood for our fire, and made down our beds with our saddles and horse-cloths.

While we were seated at supper, I proposed to my companion to go a short distance from the wood, that we might command a more extensive range of view than we could where we were seated; so that should the runaways be anywhere in the neighbourhood, we might find them out by the light of their fire. No glare appeared, however, along the whole length of the forest; but still that was no proof that they were not somewhere in one of its recesses, as, even should they have kindled a fire, the trees might conceal its light from us.

Neither of us feeling inclined for sleep, we sat up talking.

"I much regret being obliged to leave the farm, for I confess that I am not quite satisfied about the movements of the Indians who have been seen by the chief Winnemak," observed Lieutenant Broadstreet. "Should they return to the farm, your friends will be exposed to great danger. I purpose, on reaching Fort Harwood, to lay the state of the case before the commandant, and to try and induce him to send me back with a body of men, either to relieve the garrison of the farm should it be attacked, or to go in search of the marauders."

I thanked the lieutenant kindly for this offer, although I did not suppose that Uncle Jeff and his companions would have any difficulty in beating off their assailants.

"As we must be off by daylight, it is now time to turn in," said the lieutenant. "Suppose you keep one eye open, and I another! We must not, if we can help it, be surprised by wolves or bears—nor Indians either. It is just possible that the fellows whom we saw in the afternoon may follow us."

"Then I will sit up and keep watch while you sleep," I said. "If they come at all, they will try and steal upon us when they think that we may be asleep."

"I agree to your proposal," answered my companion. "If you will call me in a couple of hours, I will then take my turn, and thus let you have the morning watch. I am accustomed to have my sleep broken."

Nothing occurred during the first watch, and at the end of it I roused up the lieutenant and lay down. I suspect that he had intended to keep on watch for the rest of the night; but I happened to awake, and insisted—finding he had had a long spell—on his lying down. The young officer, therefore, rolling himself in his buffalo robe, was again quickly asleep.

I sometimes walked up and down, my rifle in my hand; sometimes leaned against a tree, peering in every direction. It could not then have wanted more than a couple of hours to dawn. The only sounds which reached my ear were those from our animals as they cropped the rich grass, or the occasional scream of some night-bird in the forest. The moon, too, was nearly at its full, and I was thus enabled to see objects at a distance distinctly. I could judge pretty well of the hour by the appearance of the fire, on which, from time to time, I threw a few sticks to keep up the blaze.

I was leaning against a tree, beginning to feel somewhat sleepy, and thinking that it would soon be time to call the lieutenant, when a sound as of something moving in the forest behind me struck on my ear. I remained perfectly motionless, and again I heard the sound. "It may be a bear," was my first thought; "but then, a bear moving among the bushes would make more noise than that. It must be some human being; perhaps an Indian, who is watching an opportunity to shoot us down."

I kept completely in the shade, while I turned my eyes in the direction from whence the sound came. I thus hoped, should there be an enemy near, to get sight of him before he could discover me.

On arousing the lieutenant, I told him of the sounds I had heard.

"If there are Indians near, we had better at once go in search of them," he answered. "I have no fancy to be shot down, as you suppose it likely we may be; and as it will not do to leave our horses, I propose that we mount them, and try and push through the forest. The moonlight will enable us to make our way without difficulty."

I should have preferred going on foot, but, of course, there was a risk, as the lieutenant had observed, of our horses being carried off. I therefore thought it wisest to agree to his proposal.

Our animals were quickly saddled, and we at once pushed into the forest. After we had passed through the outer belt, the trees grew wide apart, and as we soon came to several broad glades, we had no difficulty in making our way.

We had gone some distance, when suddenly my horse gave a start, and I caught sight of a figure, partly concealed by a tree, right ahead of me; but as I saw neither bow nor rifle-barrel, I had no fear of encountering an enemy.

"Who is there?" I asked. "Come forth and show yourself. We wish to be friends, and will not harm you."

I rode on, and just then the moonbeams, shining amid the boughs, shed their light on the figure of a young girl, whose countenance and costume plainly showed that she was an Indian. After surveying my companion and myself—apparently to ascertain who we were—she stepped forth from her place of concealment, and advanced fearlessly towards us.

"How comes it that you are wandering in this forest by yourself?" I asked.

"My friends are not far off," she answered; "and they are your friends also. I am Maysotta, the daughter of Winnemak. Seeing the light of your fire, I approached your camp, in order to ascertain who you were; but as you concealed yourself, I was unable to do so. As I had promised not to be long absent, I was returning to the camp of my people when you overtook me. My father has directed us to come on here; while he has gone back to the farm to warn your friends that the Arrapahas have once more turned their faces northward, and are very likely to carry out their hostile intentions."

"This is important information you give, Maysotta," I observed, "and we thank you for it. Are you certain if is correct?"

"My father is never deceived," she answered. "He believes that the farm will certainly be attacked, and that if those living there are not prepared, they will run a great risk of being cut off."

The lieutenant and I had dismounted, and were holding our horses by the bridle, while we talked to the Indian girl.

"If I could get hold of these deserters, I should feel warranted in returning to assist your friends," observed the lieutenant to me. "But do you think that we can depend upon the information this girl gives us?"

"I feel sure that we may," I answered. "And as I should not like to be absent while Clarice and Uncle Jeff are exposed to danger, I would certainly urge you to return. Perhaps our friend here may be able to assist us in discovering the runaways!"

I turned to Maysotta and asked her whether she or any of her people had seen the two truants, or had observed the light of a camp-fire anywhere in the forest.

"Are you seeking for any one?" she asked.

I told her that two of the lieutenant's men, forgetful of their duty, had gone off by themselves, and that they might now be of use, could they be discovered, in defending the farm.

"Will they be punished for what they have done?" she inquired.

I told the lieutenant what she said.

"Not if they return to their duty," he answered.

"Then I think I can lead you to where they are," said Maysotta. "I observed the light of a small fire reflected in the sky some little way from this, and I feel sure that it must have been kindled by the men you speak of."

"At all events, we will approach cautiously," said the lieutenant. "If my men are there, we shall have no difficulty in recovering them; or should the fire prove to be at the camp of hostile Indians, we shall be able to retreat unobserved."

Maysotta had no fear on the latter point, and advising us to picket our horses where we then were, she led the way towards the point she had described. In many places the thick foliage prevented the moonbeams from penetrating through the forest, and we could with difficulty distinguish the figure of our conductress, at so rapid a rate did she glide on through the forest.

"I hope that the girl is not deceiving us," observed the lieutenant. "Is it not possible that she may have been sent merely to beguile us into an ambush?"

"I do not think that at all likely," I answered. "There can be no doubt that she is the daughter of whom Winnemak told my sister Clarice, and that she has heard all about us from her father. She is thus anxious to render us any service in her power."

Maysotta, hearing us talking, stopped, and putting her finger to her lips, made us understand that we must be silent. She then moved forward again, at a slower pace, keeping close in front of us. After going a little farther, I observed the faint glare of a fire reflected on the loftier boughs of the trees. As we advanced it grew brighter and brighter, some of the rays penetrating even through the bushes which concealed the fire itself.

Maysotta now touched my arm, and pointing to the fallen trunk of a tree, observed, "Creep up there, and you will ascertain whether those are the people you are in search of."

We cautiously made our way towards the point indicated; but even before we could lift our heads to look over the fallen trunk, the sound of Barney Gillooly's jovial voice reached our ears, accompanied by Klitz's guttural notes.

The lieutenant was about to spring over the trunk and seize hold of the deserters at once, but I held him back.

"Let us see what the fellows are about," I whispered; and we crept closer, keeping ourselves concealed by the bushes.

Gillooly and Klitz were seated on the ground opposite each other, with the fire between them. The Irishman was holding up a piece of venison, which he had just cooked, at the end of a stick, while Klitz held another piece to the fire.

"Arrah! now, this illigint piece of meat will be enough to last us until we stop again for the night!" exclaimed Gillooly. "I'll race you now, and see who can get his whack down the fastest. If I win, you must hand over to me what remains of yours; and if you win, you shall have the remainder of my whack."

"Dat would not be fair," answered Klitz. "You got big mout and short body, and can stow away much faster dan I. You eat your breakfast as fast as you like, but let me take mine at my ease."

"Arrah! thin, here goes," cried Gillooly; and he began gnawing away with right good will at the *lump* of venison.

It was pretty evident that either he or Klitz must have

managed to kill a deer, judging from the ample supply of meat they appeared to possess. Their rifles lay at a little distance, and close to their wheel-barrow, which seemed to be well loaded. There was no danger, therefore, of their firing at us before they discovered who we were; and, besides, they were not likely men to offer any determined resistance.

We amused ourselves for some little time in watching them; and certainly no two individuals could have afforded a greater contrast. Gillooly went on eating, laughing, and drinking, diverting himself by quizzing his saturnine companion, who replied only occasionally, and in monosyllables.

"We have had enough of this," at length whispered the officer to me. "If you will seize the Irishman, I will manage the Dutchman. Hold your pistol to Gillooly's head, and he will be as quiet as a lamb. I will treat Klitz in the same way."

To bound over the trunk was the work of a moment, and the two deserters, greatly to their astonishment and dismay, found themselves in our power, without any hope of escape.

"Where were you going, you rascals?" exclaimed the lieutenant.

"Sure, your honour, a military life disagreed intirely wid me health, and I thought it best to take French leave, to save me comrades the trouble of burying me," answered Barney. "Sure, I niver dreamed of deserting."

"And you, Mr Klitz, what have you to say?" asked the lieutenant.

"Dat I could not let dis fellow, like one big baby, go alone," answered the German; "so I went to take care of him."

There was no use in bandying words just then, so the lieutenant ordering Klitz to take up the muskets, and Gillooly, as before, to trundle the wheel-barrow, we set off, guided by Maysotta, for the Indian camp.

We found but few persons in the camp, and these chiefly women and children,—the men having accompanied their chief. From the assurances Maysotta again gave us, we were convinced of the danger to which our friends were exposed. The lieutenant accordingly at once decided to leave the baggage-mules behind, and, as the Indians could supply us with a couple of horses, to mount our two men, and return at full speed to the farm.

CHAPTER FIVE

WE LEAVE THE INDIAN CAMP—MAYSOTTA'S KIND OFFER—OUR RIDE TO ROARING WATER—INDIANS IN THE DISTANCE—IN SIGHT OF THE FARM—A STRANGER INDIAN—OUR RECEPTION BY UNCLE JEFF—THE INDIAN'S STORY—HE GETS FOOD AND SHELTER—MATTERS NOW LOOK SERIOUS—A COUNCIL OF WAR—MY DOUBTS OF THE INDIAN—CLARICE AND RACHEL ACCOMPANY THE LIEUTENANT TO THE INDIAN CAMP—WE BARRICADE THE HOUSE—DISAPPEARANCE OF THE INDIAN—BARTLE GOES OUT TO RECONNOITRE—APPROACH OF THE ENEMY—A DETERMINED ATTACK—SEVERE LOSSES—THE OUT-BUILDINGS SET ON FIRE—OUR AMMUNITION RUNS SHORT—THE ROOF TAKES FIRE—HOW ARE WE TO ESCAPE?—UNCLE JEFF'S RUSE, AND HOW IT SUCCEEDED.

The Indian girl readily undertook the charge of our baggage-mules and property, as well as of the deserters' wheel-barrow, which she promised should be sent back to the farm. Having secured the muskets of the two men to our own saddles, we made them mount and ride on before us, so that they might have no opportunity of running away. Gillooly pulled as long a face as his jovial countenance was capable of, while that of Klitz elongated even more than was its wont.

"We shall probably have some sharp fighting, my lads; and if you behave well I intend to overlook your conduct; but if not, you must take the consequences," said the lieutenant.

"Sure, if we get sight of an inemy, I will do nothing to disgrace the name of Gillooly," answered Barney.

Klitz muttered something in German, but what it was I could not make out. They were neither of them likely to fight for honour and glory; at the same time, I had little doubt but they would blaze away at an enemy, when they knew that by failing to do so they would lose their scalps.

"Tell the 'Fair Lily' that I have heard of the danger by which she is threatened, and that if she will come here Maysotta will take care of her, and cherish her as a sister," said the Indian girl, as I was about to vault into my saddle.

I thanked her, and told her that I was sure Clarice would be glad to meet with her. I was much struck by the artless manners of the young Indian girl, who, although endowed with the features of her race, possessed a beauty rarely seen among them.

"Move on, lads; we must be at Roaring Water before nightfall," cried the lieutenant. "Keep together, and do not pull rein until I give the order. Remember that I will stand no nonsense; and the first of you who plays any trick, I will shoot him through the head."

"Arrah! sure, we will be afther obeying your honour, thin," cried Barney, as he and Klitz galloped on ahead—the lieutenant giving them the order to turn to the right or to the left as was necessary.

We kept on at a good pace. The Indian mustangs, although somewhat small, were strong and wiry; and our horses, having had a good feed, were perfectly fresh. The distance, therefore, which on the previous days—having our mules to drag after us—was slowly traversed, was now quickly got over. But we had to call a halt at noon, by the side of a stream, in order to water our animals and let them feed; while we ourselves took some of the provender which we had brought in our wallets.

Klitz and Barney sat down opposite to us, by the orders of the lieutenant, and ate their meal in silence. They bore their disappointment very well. Perhaps, after their three or four days' experience, they may have begun to suspect that they would not reach their El Dorado without some considerable difficulty, should they ever get there at all; and they possibly consoled themselves with the idea that, since they had been retaken, they were getting off very cheaply.

Our meal over, we moved on as before. I kept a sharp look-out by the way, and twice I caught sight of figures which I knew must be Indians, moving in the distance, but whether friends or foes it was impossible to say. Perhaps they belonged to Winnemak's tribe; or, should Maysotta's account be correct, they might be Arrapahas. They did not approach us, however, and we were allowed to proceed unmolested.

Although we were moving along the line used by emigrant trains, we did not meet a single one; but it was possible that any coming from the eastward might have been attacked by the Arrapahas, or, hearing that an enemy was in the neighbourhood, might have halted for the purpose of defending themselves. When Indians can manage to attack a train on the move, they, in most instances, prove successful; whereas even a small party of white men, when encamped and under the protection of their waggons, can generally keep a large band of warriors at bay.

The fact of our not meeting with any emigrant trains made Maysotta's report more probable. Of course I felt somewhat anxious about ourselves, for, even although we had a couple of rifles and two muskets, besides our pistols, we might find it a hard matter to drive off any large number of mounted assailants; but I felt far more anxious about the inmates of the farm.

We kept the two men moving ahead of us at such a rate that Barney more than once cried out, "Sure, lieutenant, our bastes will have no wind left in thim at all, at all, if we don't pull up!"

"Go on, go on," cried the lieutenant; "do not mind your beasts, as long as they can keep their legs."

"Thin it's meself I'd be plading for," cried Barney, turning round.

"Do not mind yourself either," answered the lieutenant. "The lives of our friends are at stake, and if we are to help them we must get to the farm without delay."

Whack, whack, whack went Barney's stick. The German also urged forward his mustang in the same manner—his feet, from the length of his legs, nearly touching the ground. Indeed, when passing through long grass, his feet were so completely hidden, that, as he kept moving his legs about all the time, it appeared as if he were running along with his horse under him.

At length the mountains which rose above Roaring Water appeared in sight. As we neared them I looked out eagerly from the summit of a ridge we had reached, to ascertain if any Indians were in the neighbourhood; but as none were to be seen, I hoped that we might reach the farm before any attack had been commenced.

As we passed the confines of the property I saw none of our people about; but, as the evening was drawing on, I thought it probable that they had gone home from their work. Still, I felt somewhat anxious; my anxiety being also shared by the lieutenant, who was making his tired beast breast the hill faster than he, as a humane man, would otherwise have done.

As we got close to the house, an Indian started up from behind a copse which grew on the side of the hill. He had neither war-paint nor ornaments on, and looked weary and travel-stained. He was a young, active man; but, at the first glance, I did not like his countenance. A person unaccustomed to Indians cannot easily distinguish one from another, although in reality they vary in appearance as much as white men do; as does also the expression of their countenances.

"Are you going to the farm?" he asked, addressing me. He knew at once by my dress that I was a settler.

"Yes," I replied. "Why do you put the question?"

"I wish to go there too," he answered. "I want to tell the Palefaces living there that they are likely to be attacked by enemies who have sworn to take their scalps, and that unless they run away they will all lose their lives."

"You do not bring us news," I replied; "but you can accompany us to the farm and speak to the white chief, telling him what you know—although I do not think it likely that he will follow your advice."

"Come on, come on, Ralph," cried the lieutenant; "do not lose time by talking to that fellow."

I quickly overtook my companion; while the Indian followed, notwithstanding his tired appearance, at a speed which soon brought him up with us.

As we rode up to the house, Uncle Jeff appeared at the door.

"What has brought you back?" he exclaimed, with a look of surprise. "Glad to see you, at all events; for we have had our friend Winnemak here with news sufficient to make our hair stand on end, if it were addicted to anything of that sort. He declares that the Arrapahas are coming on in overwhelming force, and that, unless we are well prepared for them, we shall one and all of us lose our scalps. He has gone off again, though, promising to make a diversion in our favour, as he has been unable to get his people to come and assist in defending the farm, which would have been more to the purpose. However, as you have returned,—and brought your two deserters, I see,—we shall be able to beat the varmints off. No fear of it, though they may be as thick as a swarm of bees."

A few words explained how we had fallen in with the runaways.

The Indian who accompanied us then stepped forward. He told Uncle Jeff that he was a Pawnee, that his name was Piomingo, and that, having a warm affection for the Palefaces, he had come to warn us of the danger in which we were placed, and to advise us forthwith to desert the farm and take to the mountains, for that we had not a chance of defending it against the numerous bands of Arrapahas who were advancing to attack us. They had, he said, put to death all the white men, as well as women and children, they had met with in their progress, as their manner was to spare no one; and they would certainly treat us in the same way.

"We have already heard something of this," said Uncle Jeff, looking as unconcerned as he could; "but how did you happen to know about it?" he asked.

"I was taken prisoner by the Arrapahas while on my way to visit a young squaw, who is to become my wife. But on the night before I was to be tortured and put to death I managed to make my escape, and came on here at once to tell the Palefaces of their danger, of which I had heard when in the camp of the enemy."

I suspected that Uncle Jeff did not altogether believe the account given by the Indian. At any rate, he received it with perfect composure.

"We thank you, friend Piomingo, for your good intentions. You are now at liberty to pursue your journey on your intended visit to the young squaw of whom you speak," he answered.

"I would follow the advice of the Paleface chief, but I am weary and hungry, and require sleep and rest. He would not turn me away like a dog from his door!"

"No, I will not do that," said Uncle Jeff. "You shall have as much food as you require, and you can lie down and sleep until you are rested; after that, you shall be welcome to depart."

The Indian expressed his gratitude in a much longer speech than the occasion required; but when Rachel brought some food he ate it voraciously, as if he really were as hungry as he had asserted.

Clarice blushed and smiled, when the lieutenant told her how anxious he had been made by the report he had received from Maysotta, and how glad he was for the opportunity of returning.

The sergeant was by this time much better, and able to move about. Pat, too, had behaved very well. The four farm hands had been brought into the house, and Sergeant Custis and Pat had been regularly drilling them, and teaching them how to handle their muskets properly.

I found that Uncle Jeff considered matters far more serious than he had at first been willing to do. Winnemak had been urging him to allow Clarice, attended by Rachel, to quit the farm—promising to conduct them to his daughter, and to afford them protection. Should the farm be attacked, it was quite possible that the defenders might have, as a last resource, to cut their way out; and, encumbered with the two women, the risk they would have to run would be far greater than if they had only themselves to think of.

"I cannot help acknowledging that our Indian friend's advice is sound," observed Uncle Jeff. "If we knew that Clarice and Rachel were safe, we should fight with far more freedom than we could do with them in the house. And if matters came to the worst, we should, as he says, be able to escape with far less difficulty than if we had them to look after."

"I am very unwilling to desert you," said the lieutenant; "but, under the circumstances, if you will confide your niece to my care, with her attendant, I will undertake to escort them to the Indian camp, where the chief's daughter is ready to receive her. Indeed, the Indian girl proposed this herself, and seemed to be aware of what her father had advised you to do."

While we were talking, I observed that the stranger was listening, and apparently doing his best to take in what we said. Though he was a handsome young fellow, yet, as I before remarked, I did not like the expression of his countenance; it now struck me that it had a cunning, sinister look. Whenever he saw my eyes directed towards him, he turned away, and appeared to be thinking only of the food he was eating.

I have elsewhere alluded to my talent as an artist. While Winnemak was with us, I had made a tolerably fair portrait of him; indeed, it was considered a good likeness, and was hung up against the wall. As Piomingo was passing it, I saw him start in a way an Indian seldom does; and he then stood gazing earnestly at it for a minute or more.

"Who is that man?" he asked, pointing to the portrait.

I told him.

"Ah, bad man!" he muttered; "take care what he do."

"We think him a good man; he is a friend of ours."

He shook his head, but said nothing more. After this, instead of lying down, he stole near to where Uncle Jeff, the lieutenant, and I were talking; although, unless he knew English much better than he seemed to do, he could not have been any the wiser.

Uncle Jeff considered seriously the proposal made by Winnemak, and now repeated by the lieutenant.

"Yes," he said at length, "I am sure it is the best plan. I will entrust my niece and Rachel to your charge. I conclude you will take your men with you! Indeed, although we can ill spare any hands, I wish Ralph to accompany you, if you will allow him."

"You may trust me, Mr Crockett, that I will defend your niece and her attendant with my life; but I shall be very glad to have the aid of your nephew," answered Lieutenant Broadstreet. "With regard to my own men, I propose taking only the most trustworthy, Sergeant Custis and Sperry; the other two I will leave with you, for they will, at all events, fight as well as better men within walls, and I can more readily spare them than the others."

On hearing this arrangement, I was placed in a dilemma. I did not at all like the idea of being compelled to quit the post of danger; while at the same time I felt it was my duty to assist in protecting Clarice. I told the lieutenant how I felt on the subject.

"I will speak to your uncle," he answered; "and if you wish to remain, I will assure him that your coming is not absolutely necessary. We may hope to reach the Indian camp early to-morrow, and your sister will then be placed under the charge of the Indian chief and his daughter."

When I put the question to Clarice, she replied,—"I would infinitely rather have you with me; but if you believe that it is your duty to remain with Uncle Jeff, I could not bear the thought of your leaving him. Besides, he seems to be confident that he will be able to beat off the enemy, should the farm be attacked."

I confess that I was in two minds on the subject until the last moment.

The plans being arranged, no time was lost in making the necessary preparations. The horses which had been selected for the journey having been well fed and watered, were brought to the door. Clarice was soon ready. She was a good horse-woman, and even Rachel had been accustomed to the saddle in former years.

I wrung my friend's hand.

"You will take care of my sister, I know you will," I said as I parted from him.

"Indeed, Ralph, I will," he answered solemnly; and I felt that she was as safe as she would have been had I accompanied her.

The moon was now shining brightly, and enabled the lieutenant and his companions to pursue their way at a rapid rate. They took no baggage except such as could be strapped to the saddles of their horses; they were, therefore, not impeded as we had been by slow-moving mules. It was nearly midnight when they set off; and as little noise as possible was made when they left the house, in case any of the enemy's scouts watching in the neighbourhood might hear them.

The stranger Indian had, some time before the party set off, thrown himself on a buffalo robe in a corner of the room, and was apparently asleep; but I suspected that he knew pretty well all that was going forward. He remained, however, without moving, as if in a sound slumber.

As soon as Uncle Jeff and I returned (we had accompanied our friends a little way down the hill), Uncle Jeff addressed his small garrison.

"Putting all things together, lads," said he, "I believe these Redskin varmints whom we have been hearing of for some days past will really at last make an attempt to rob the farm; but I know that you will fight to the last, and we shall manage to drive them off. There is no reason why we should not feel confident of success. We have a good store of powder and bullets, with trustworthy rifles and muskets; and what more, pray, can men wish for?"

The men, one and all, promised to stand by him.

"That is all I want," he answered. "The first thing we have to do is to barricade the lower windows and the doors, so that while we are defending one side the Indians may not walk in at the other."

There were ten of us altogether, and having abundance of tools and materials, we soon put the building in a state of defence, with loopholes on all sides. Before the doors were finally closed, Uncle Jeff told Bartle to bring in his favourite horse "Jack;" the remainder of the animals had been turned loose to seek their own safety.

The day dawned, but as nothing had yet been seen of our expected enemies, Bartle agreed to go out and ascertain their whereabouts as soon as the sun rose above the horizon. Bartle was too old a scout to care whether he had to approach an enemy in daylight or darkness; his only object at present was to find out if the Indians were really marching towards the farm.

While we were busily engaged in barricading the house, no one had thought of our Redskin visitor. When last seen he was apparently wrapped in slumber.

"I suppose we may count on Piomingo as one of the

defenders of the house; he probably knows how to use a rifle," observed Uncle Jeff, near whom I was working. "Go and speak to him. Say that we expect him to do his duty; and ask him if he knows how to load a rifle."

As soon as I had finished the work I was about, I went to where Piomingo had been lying down. He was not there; I looked everywhere about for him, but he had disappeared. No one had seen him leave the house, so that, if he was not still within, he must have watched his opportunity when our eyes were off him, and slipped out.

What his object was in coming, and then going away secretly, it was difficult to say. His departure was suspicious, too; he might have visited us with treacherous intentions. But perhaps he was merely a coward, and finding that we would not take his advice and desert the farm, he had escaped, to avoid the danger to which he would be exposed. However, if he intended treachery, it was better to have him out of the way.

"Maybe, afther all, the spalpeen is hiding somewhere," observed Gillooly, when he found that we were inquiring for the Indian; "if he is anywhere inside, sure I'll ferret him out;" and the Irishman immediately began poking his nose into every hole and cranny in the building.

"Bedad! he's convarted himself into a rat, for nowhere can I find him in any hole that a mortal man could stow himself into!" exclaimed Barney, after a long search.

I have not yet described the building which, if we were attacked, was to serve as our fortress. It was of considerable size; the lower part of the walls consisting of stout logs, the upper portion being of framework, and boarded. Round three sides was a stout palisade, forming an enclosure, while the remaining side was occupied by stables and other out-buildings. Barns, cow-sheds, and piggeries were placed at some little distance off. Then there was the hut occupied by the farm hands; while overhanging the stream, which flowed by on one side, was a small mill, the wheel of which was turned by its waters.

The hills rose on either side, but too far off to allow an enemy to command the house from them; while the intervening space was rough and rocky,—forming shelter, however, to an approaching foe. Had we felt sure that we would be attacked, we should have been wise to have destroyed many of these out-buildings, as they were calculated to protect the enemy. But to the last Uncle Jeff was not fully persuaded that the Indians would venture to approach the place, as they must have known that we were prepared for their reception.

The day drew on, but still Bartle did not return; and we began to hope that after all no enemy would appear. But about noon, and just as we were making ready to sit down to dinner, he was seen approaching the house with rapid strides.

"There is no doubt about what these varmints intend!" he exclaimed as he rushed into the house. "They are coming on as fast as their legs can carry them, and will be here before the day is much older. Look to your firearms, lads; we must be ready for them, and give them such a dose of bullets that they will wish they hadn't come to Roaring Water."

In accordance with Bartle's advice, all the doors and windows were fast closed, and we were shut up in our fortress.

"It is ill to fight on empty stomachs, so turn to and eat your dinner, lads; I'll give you notice when you are wanted."

Uncle Jeff having thus spoken, mounted to a window commanding the road by which the enemy were likely to approach; and there, after snatching a hasty meal, I quickly joined him. I first, however, took a glance out of another window, opening to the southward, as it was possible that some of the Indians might make their way over the hills so as to take us on the flank.

To each man was given his particular post, at which he was to remain until summoned elsewhere.

The time now seemed to go by very slowly.

"I do not think they will come, after all," I observed to Uncle Jeff; "more than an hour has passed since Bartle returned."

He looked at his watch. "It is not one o'clock yet," he observed; "and Bartle does not often make a mistake."

Just as he spoke, I saw the plumes of a chief's head-dress rising over a point of rocky ground round which the road passed, and shortly afterwards a band of painted warriors came into view. They approached very cautiously, and gazed about them, as if expecting at any moment to encounter an enemy. Finding, however, that none of us were visible, they began to advance at a more rapid rate. Immediately afterwards I saw another and a much larger party coming over the hill, who, as they drew near, scattered themselves in every direction, so as to be able to get under shelter behind the intervening rocks and shrubs.

"Tell the men to be ready," cried Uncle Jeff; "and charge them not to fire until I give the word,—they must not throw a shot away."

I ran hastily round the building, and ascertained that every man was at his post, prepared for whatever might happen. I then returned to Uncle Jeff for further orders.

Presently an Indian belonging to the party which had descended the hill advanced towards the house with a white handkerchief on a pole.

"The fellows have some pretensions to civilisation," said Uncle Jeff when he saw it; "perhaps their white friends have put them up to that."

The Indian, having got within speaking distance, now halted; but seeing no one whom he could address, he proceeded around the building, apparently examining our preparations for defence. At length he again stopped, having satisfied himself that the building was fortified, and contained a garrison.

"Friends," he shouted, "do you want to lose your scalps? If not, march out and leave this house to us. We mean to come in."

Uncle Jeff now appeared at the window opposite to where the Indian was standing.

"Clear out of this, you rascal!" he exclaimed. "We do not intend that you shall have our scalps, or get inside these walls. If you make the attempt, you will pay dearly for it; that is what I've got to say."

The Indian seemed to recognise Uncle Jeff. "You, Jeff Crockett," he shouted out, "you good man! If you like to go out you may go, and we take scalps of rest."

Uncle Jeff burst into a loud laugh.

"That's a likely thing," he thundered out. "If it was not for your white flag, I would treat you as you deserve."

The tone of voice in which this was said convinced the Indian that Uncle Jeff was in earnest; and in no very dignified fashion he scampered off to rejoin his companions.

The whole of the band now united in giving utterance to a terrific war-whoop, and came rushing up to the house. There was no longer any doubt as to their intentions; they halted for a moment to fire, and then came right on at a rapid pace, up to the palisade.

"Now, lads, give it them!" shouted Uncle Jeff; and every bullet fired by our little garrison brought down one of our foes.

The death of their companions served but to inflame the rage of the rest; and climbing up over the palisade of which I have spoken, they attempted to get into the enclosure. Several were shot down in the act; but others succeeded in reaching the enclosure, though they soon paid dearly for their activity, as they were shot down as soon as we could reload our rifles. The loss of so many men in their first attack seemed to discourage the rest, and they drew off to a distance, under such shelter as they could find.

"We have soon settled the fellows; they have had enough of it," cried some of our men.

"Wait a bit, lads," said Bartle; "that is not the Indian fashion. They will be upon us again before long."

He was right; in a few minutes a considerable number of the enemy were seen moving round, in order to get to the rear of the out-buildings—Bartle and Gideon meanwhile picking off two or three who incautiously exposed themselves. Having gained the position they desired, they made a rush towards the buildings, which sheltered them almost entirely from our fire. Breaking through the enclosure on that side, they next advanced boldly into the open space in front of the stables, where they were once more exposed to view. Scarcely had they reached it when Bartle's unerring rifle brought down their leader. His followers, on seeing this, rushed into the stables, while others made their appearance in the same direction.

Either because they fancied that their chief was still alive, or that it was a disgrace to allow his body to remain on the ground, a couple of warriors dashed out for the purpose of carrying it off; but before they had time to stoop down and lift it from the ground, Gideon and Bartle's rifles had laid them both by its side. Two others followed, and were picked off by Gillooly and Klitz, both of whom showed themselves no despicable shots. In the meantime Bartle and Gideon had reloaded, and two more warriors shared the fate of the first.

As yet, all the success had been on our side; and there appeared every probability of our being able to defeat any attempt of the enemy to enter the building. Those who had got into the stables were so many withdrawn from the attack; and although under shelter, they could effect nothing against us. Had the Indians been alone, we might have kept them at bay, cunning as they were; but there were white men among them, who, although not eager to expose their own lives, were well able to assist our enemies by their advice.

Presently our assailants, with the exception of those in the stables and other out-buildings, retreated. It was but for a short time, however; soon they appeared on the opposite side of the house, many of them carrying burning brands, which they threw under the fencing. This being of combustible materials, soon blazed up; and, sheltered by the intervening flames and smoke, the enemy opened a hot fire on us. Every now and then, however, a dark form was seen, and as surely a bullet searched it out. But the whole of our little garrison was now required to keep the enemy at bay on this side; and those who had been hidden in the out-buildings took the opportunity of making their escape. Some of them, we found, had thrown themselves into the mill, which afforded them sufficient shelter to fire steadily at our loopholes with less risk of being hit in return. None of us had hitherto been struck, but no sooner had the mill been taken possession of than two of the farm hands, who were less cautious than the experienced hunters, were badly wounded—one of them mortally, while the other was unable to handle his rifle.

The palisade being now burned to the ground, we were deprived of its protection, and our assailants could consequently get close up to the walls. But though our numbers were diminished, we endeavoured, by the rapidity of our fire, not to let the enemy discover our loss.

The fight had now continued for some hours, but still our foes seemed as determined as ever to capture the place. They, or perhaps the white men, had heard a report that Uncle Jeff was the owner of fabulous wealth, of which they had resolved to make themselves the possessors. This would account for their obstinate perseverance.

Fresh bands continued to arrive, too; and after a cessation of firing, a shower of arrows, from enemies concealed behind the rocks, came flying over the house. Had they been simply arrows, they would not have done much harm; but, to our dismay, we saw that each one carried a piece of burning tow; and if these fell on the shingles of the roof, they would too probably set them on fire. To extinguish the flames, too, we should have to expose ourselves to a great risk of being shot.

Happily, as yet the arrows either flew over the building, or the tow fell out, and as far as we could discover no damage had been done. Some, however, struck the out-buildings; and the roofs of these being thatched, they were soon in flames. The barns, too, were set on fire, and blazed furiously.

Night at length came on, but it brought us no respite; for our savage foes could be seen, by the light from the burning out-buildings, still hovering in vast numbers round us. Suddenly, too, the granary burst into flames, making the night almost as bright as the day. It enabled us, however, to see our foes more clearly, and of this we did not fail to take advantage. We prudently retained only light enough in the house to enable us to see our way about; and we were thus comparatively concealed, while they were exposed to view.

We might have still kept the enemy at bay, had not the other two field hands both been struck down, in the same manner as their companions. We were now only six, opposed, as it appeared to us, to several hundred foes. Still no one dreamed of giving in.

Klitz and Gillooly behaved admirably, and did much to retrieve their character. They always kept together—Klitz kneeling down to fire, while Gillooly sprang now on one side, then on the other, of his loophole, as he fired his rifle through it.

Our position had become very critical; the wind might at any moment bring the flames of the out-buildings against the house itself, in which case our fate would be sealed, for it would be almost impossible for us to extinguish them.

At length, to our relief, the enemy again drew off. From their previous daring conduct, we could not hope, however, that they intended to raise the siege; perhaps they only waited to see whether the flames from the out-buildings would set the house on fire, and thus save them all further trouble and danger. But the wind, fortunately, continued to blow up the valley, keeping the flames away from the house.

Uncle Jeff now directed me to go round and give some food to each man. When I came to him, "Ralph," said he, "go and look into the ammunition-chest. I have my fears that we are running short of cartridges!"

I did as directed, and what was my dismay to find that no more than three rounds remained for each one of us! One of the poor fellows who had been last hit had been employed in supplying us with cartridges, and he had omitted to tell Uncle Jeff how short we had run.

"I wish I had let you go, Ralph," he said; "but it cannot be helped now. We must cut our way out; it is possible that all of us who are alive may succeed. If the enemy come on again, we must begin blazing away at them as before; then, when our last shot is expended, we must burst open the door and dart out. Call Bartle and Gideon, and I will tell them what I propose doing. You and they are active, and know the country, and if you can reach the mountains you may get off free; although it will go hard, I fear, with the two troopers."

His two old followers, on hearing that the ammunition was almost expended, agreed that it was the only course to pursue with any chance of saving our lives.

Fortunately there were several swords, and we each of us provided ourselves with one, and besides this we had a pistol apiece.

"Now, then," said Uncle Jeff, "I propose doing what will look like deserting you, but in reality it is the best plan for saving your lives. I am thinking of dressing up a figure, and placing it on Jack's back, so as to partly cover me when I am mounted; and I will conceal myself by hanging over along his neck. I will then dash out ahead of you, when the enemy are certain to direct their fire at me, though I hope that they will hit the figure instead. You, in the meantime, can make up the valley; and as you know every inch of the ground, you will soon distance them. What say you to my proposal, Bartle?"

"It is as good as any I can think of," answered Bartle. "I wish you would let me ride the horse, though, for I think you run a greater risk than any of us."

"No, no," answered Uncle Jeff; "although that may be true, it is my duty to you all. And Jack knows me better than any one else; it won't be his fault if he doesn't carry me clear."

I at once began to consider how I could make such a figure as would answer Uncle Jeff's purpose, and as I was of an ingenious turn, I was not long, with the aid of some pliable laths and some strips of cow-hide, in making the framework; the arms I formed in the attitude of holding the reins. The framework once formed, it was quickly clothed in the costume generally worn by Uncle Jeff; and as I placed it with the legs over a chair, it was allowed that, on a dark night, it might deceive those not prepared for the trick to be played upon them.

Jack, who had been busy munching his hay in a corner of the room, was now saddled, and the figure placed in position, and secured with straps round the body; while Uncle Jeff himself, stripped to his trousers, hung over in the attitude he proposed. Looking across the dimly-lighted room, we could scarcely perceive him.

"That will do," cried Bartle enthusiastically; "it will give you a better chance of escape, at all events."

We had reason to be thankful that the Indians gave us so long a time for preparation. The night was now advancing, and any doubts that we might have entertained as to their having taken their departure were soon dissipated, for once more showers of fiery arrows came flying over and against the house—shot, however, from a distance. Several whistled through the loopholes, but none of us were hit, and these were of course immediately extinguished.

I was in the upper story, when, looking up, to my dismay I saw a bright light overhead; the roof had been set on fire. Under other circumstances we might have attempted to extinguish it; as it was, I ran to tell Uncle Jeff what had occurred.

"Then the time has come, my lads, when we must cut our way out. God protect one and all of us. Would that I could help you further."

We shook hands round, and Bartle and Gideon stood by with their axes to knock away the barricade. Uncle Jeff mounted Jack, and secured the figure behind him. Some time passed, however, before he gave the word. The enemy were close at hand, but they were concentrated, as far as we could judge by the sounds which reached us, on one side of the house, and Uncle Jeff would be able to pass by them, and thus leave the road open for us.

A few strokes cleared away the barricade. Uncle Jeff was to dash out first, Bartle and Gideon were to follow, they understanding that I should keep between them, while Klitz and Gillooly were to bring up the rear.

"Now open the door!" cried Uncle Jeff.

Just as he spoke I looked around, and discovered that neither Klitz nor Gillooly was behind me. What had become of them I could not tell; and there was no time to consider, for the door was thrown open, and out dashed Uncle Jeff, directing his course by the path down the valley.

For some seconds he was not observed by the enemy, until he went clattering away down the steep path at a pace which would have brought many a steed on his knees. But Jack knew what he was about. Not until Uncle Jeff found that the enemy had seen him did he utter a sound. He then gave vent to a loud shout, which rang through the air, echoing from rock to rock. It had the effect he intended, and drew the attention of our foes to him. A shower of bullets went whistling through the figure and on either side of it; still the horse kept on his way uninjured.

The Indians, who had their horses tethered below, mounted in haste, and pushed on in hot chase. But Uncle Jeff was on ahead of them, so, casting off the straps which bound the figure, he let it fall to the ground, whilst he, recovering his proper position, turned round, and shaking his fist at his astonished foes, continued his course at increased speed.

We of course could not see what occurred, but we heard of it afterwards.

CHAPTER SIX

WE ARE SURPRISED BY THE INDIANS WHILE LEAVING THE HOUSE—BARTLE'S ADVICE—I AM PERSUADED TO ESCAPE ALONE—AN EXCITING PURSUIT—FOOD AND REST—MY JOURNEY RESUMED—AMONG THE MOUNTAINS—MY ANXIETY ABOUT MY FRIENDS—A WEARY DAY—AN INDIAN IN SIGHT—FRIEND OR ENEMY?—A RECOGNITION—WINNEMAK AND HIS BRAVES—I AM KINDLY TREATED—NO NEWS OF UNCLE JEFF—A SPY—WE START IN PURSUIT OF HIM—THE SPY OVERTAKEN—A DEADLY COMBAT—WINNEMAK OVERCOMES PIOMINGO—IS HE DEAD?—MY INTERCESSION—ON THE WAY FOR WINNEMAK'S CAMP.

The furious rush made by Uncle Jeff had, as he expected, so distracted the attention of our numerous enemies surrounding the house, that they did not at first notice Bartle, Gideon, and me. We were thus able to get to some distance from the house, and had hopes of escaping altogether unobserved, when the party who had been concealed in the mill caught sight of us, and uttering a loud war-whoop, rushed out expecting to take our scalps. Bartle and Gideon shot down with their pistols two of our assailants; and I cut down a third, who had sprung before us to stop our progress. Others soon came on, but we managed to keep them at bay, although it was too probable that ere long we should be overwhelmed, as others were coming up from all directions to join the fight. But so well did my companions wield their swords, that they for some time kept the enemy back.

"Now, lad," cried Bartle to me, "now is your time; run for it, and you will get off free! Gideon and I will manage these fellows; never fear, we will look after ourselves."

I hesitated to desert my faithful friends.

"Go, I say—go, Ralph!" again cried Bartle. "It will make it more difficult for us to escape if you remain."

It was probable, I saw, that Bartle and Gideon, with their great strength and activity, might by themselves be able to cut their way through a host of foes, although with me to protect they might find the task too great even for them.

"Good-bye, then; I hope we shall meet all right before long," I exclaimed.

"Never fear, lad," cried Bartle, as I bounded off up the canon, my rifle at my back, with three spare cartridges, and my pistol in my belt.

For some seconds the Indians did not observe what I was about, and I soon had a good start of them. When at length they did catch sight of my figure, dimly seen in the gloom of early morning, for it was scarcely yet daylight, several started off in chase. I saw that they were coming, but I did not stop to count their number. I was well acquainted with every inch of the ground, which it was not likely that they were, and I knew I should have abundance of hiding-places between the rocks and crags, among which I might baffle pursuit. My purpose then was to cross the torrent at a narrow part where a tree hung over it, and to make to the northward, where I hoped to join Uncle Jeff and Clarice at Winnemak's camp.

The Indians, however, had no intention of allowing me to escape. On they came, uttering loud shrieks and shouts, expecting to strike terror into my heart, and make me yield. Two or three were in advance of the rest, and one especially seemed to be gaining on me. I would not willingly have taken his life, but too probably, should I not stop his progress, he would take mine. Having reached a rock, I sprang behind it; then unslinging my rifle, I stepped out and took steady aim at the advancing foe, who fell back shot through the body. His fall had the effect of stopping the others, who lifted him up to ascertain if he were dead, thus affording me time to reload my rifle, and gain several more yards in advance. I could thus bring down another enemy, if necessary, at a distance, and still have my pistol and sword to defend myself in a closer encounter.

I had not forgotten my two brave friends. I only wished that they had accompanied me, for we might, on the ground I had now reached, have set a whole host of our enemies at defiance.

I sprang on among the rocks, almost entirely concealed from the view of my pursuers. Few of them, fortunately, had firearms, although an occasional ill-aimed bullet whistled over my head, but I had very little fear of being struck while among the rocks. My great object was to reach the tree over the torrent before the Indians came up, because I should be exposed to view when climbing along the trunk.

I dashed on, and mounting the rock still unobserved, reached the root of the tree. It would be necessary to use great caution as I approached the further end, as only the more delicate branches hung over the stream, and should I venture on one incapable of bearing my weight I should fall into the torrent, which there went roaring by at a fearful rate. This very circumstance, however, should I succeed, would secure my safety, as, even should the Indians discover by what means I had crossed, they would not venture to follow; or if they did, would most probably fall into the current and be swept away.

I did not stop to ascertain how far off my pursuers were, but, climbing up on the trunk, I made my way along it—trusting to the uncertainty of their aim, should any with muskets see me and fire. My great object was now to discover a bough on which I could depend. I cast my eye along one, as far as the light would allow, and selected it; then, like a wild cat about to spring on its prey, I crawled quickly on. There were several branches below me, which, should the one I was on give way, would still afford me support, and there were many on either side. The bough bent with my weight, and as I reached the further end I every moment expected that it would break. I felt it giving way, cracking horribly. It broke! I endeavoured to seize another bough—in vain. With a crash, down I came, but it was to find myself on the opposite bank, and by making a few springs I reached the upper ground.

On looking back to ascertain if the Indians had found out the way by which I had crossed, I could see no one, but I caught sight in the distance of a bright glare, which I was too certain was caused by our burning house, every part of which by this time must have been in flames. I did not stop, however, to contemplate the sad scene, but pushed on as fast as I was able. I could not trust to the Indians not pursuing me, for I knew, when intent on an object, that they will run every danger rather than abandon it, and the death of their companion would make them still more eager to kill me than might otherwise have been the case. On, therefore, I sprang. I could still hear them, although I believed they had not seen me cross by the tree, or perhaps even had not discovered the tree itself, as it was concealed by an intervening rock. I hoped that they would fancy I had taken the way further up the canon, and would pursue in that direction. I might therefore proceed at a less furious pace than I had hitherto been going. Still, I resolved to leave nothing to chance, but to follow my course until the Indians had given up the pursuit.

Stopping to listen a moment, I could hear their voices. Again I went on as fast as before. Now I had a mountain to scale; now to make my way along its steep side; now to descend into a valley; now to wade across a stream which threatened to carry me off my legs; now to climb another height: and so on I went, until I was conscious that my strength was failing me. At length, completely exhausted, I sank down beneath an overhanging rock. It afforded me some shelter from the fiery rays of the sun, which had now risen high in the sky.

I had drunk at a spring on my way, but I again felt painfully thirsty. Could I obtain some water, I should be greatly relieved; but I was not likely to find it without further exertion, and of that I was incapable. I had brought a little food in my wallet, according to Uncle Jeff's advice before we left the house, and this I believe was the means of saving my life. Although it was dry, it gave me some strength.

I remained in a sort of stupor, scarcely conscious of what had occurred; and some hours, I suspect, went by, before I attempted to resume my journey. I had no desire to spend the night in this exposed part of the mountains. The scenery around Roaring Water was wild enough, but this appeared to me wilder still. Lofty broken cliffs rose on either side of me.

So broken and irregular were their fantastic forms, that I could fancy myself amid the ruins of some Egyptian temple. It seemed to be a gateway, as it were, to some still wilder or more wonderful region, as yet unexplored by the foot of man. I had never been thus far before, and had very just fears, should darkness come on, of losing my way. I therefore pushed forward as fast as my strength would allow, in the hope of coming upon water, and kept a sharp look-out in every direction to find indication of it.

The sun had crossed the mountains, and was sinking towards the west; in a short time the shadows of their peaks would be thrown over the ground upon which I was travelling. Stopping for a moment, I heard the sound of water rushing over a rocky bed, and hurrying forward I found myself beside a foaming stream. I had, however, to seek for a path by which I could descend, before I could slake my thirst. At last I got to a place where, lying at full length, and holding on with one hand by the branch of a bush, I could lift the water with the other to my mouth. It seemed impossible to get enough; but at last I felt that I ought to take no more.

The ground being tolerably practicable along the bank of the stream, I proceeded in that direction, desirous of reaching a lower region before nightfall; and as I went along I resolved to seek for some bushes or an overhanging rock, under which to take shelter for the night.

I had now very little fear of being overtaken; indeed, the Indians would probably have lost my trail in the streams I had crossed, while the rocky nature of the ground would scarcely bear marks sufficient for even their acute eyes to discover. I knew that as yet I could not be abreast of Winnemak's camp, and, indeed, that across the mountains it would probably take me two or three days to reach it. Still I felt that it would be prudent, in case the Indians should be scouring the country in the plains, to keep to the mountains for another whole day or so.

Just at dusk I saw a spot at which, from the appearance of the water, I judged that I could cross the torrent. "I will put that, at all events, between myself and my enemies, should they be pursuing me," I thought, and without further hesitation I waded towards the opposite shore. The water rose higher and higher. I had, I feared, been deceived by the light, and might have to swim for it. The danger of this was, that I might lose my rifle, and wet my pistol and ammunition. Very thankful, therefore, was I when the water again shallowed; and, keeping my feet in spite of the rush against my legs, I at last got to the bank to which I was directing my course.

I now continued down the stream until I reached a rock which almost overhung it, with bushes on either side. This, I saw, would afford me as secure a resting-place as I could expect to find. I accordingly resolved to stop; and having examined the locality on the further side, in case I should have to beat a retreat, I sat down and took some food, of which I still had a small portion left. The air was tolerably warm, and, fatigued as I was, I should under ordinary circumstances have slumbered soundly; but as it was I felt very little inclination to sleep. I was too anxious about Uncle Jeff, and Bartle, and Gideon. Had Uncle Jeff escaped the bullets of the enemy; and had the others managed to cut their way through the horde of savages? The white men in company with the Redskins, I looked upon as no better than they were. What, too, had become of the German and the Irishman? Had they, afraid of fighting in the open, remained in the house, and fallen victims to the flames? Such, indeed, must have been the fate of the poor wounded fellows left in the house. My only satisfaction was, that we had done all that men could do, and that we could not have saved their lives, although we should, to a certainty, have sacrificed our own had we made the attempt. Still I had an idea that Barney and Klitz had some plan of their own for escaping, and that they might turn up some day or other. I half expected to find that Bartle and Gideon had followed me, and I looked out eagerly, hoping to see them. How far I had come I could not exactly calculate, but I knew that, at the rate I had been moving, it must be a considerable distance.

At length, overcome by fatigue, I fell asleep, trusting that He by whom I had been mercifully preserved would watch over me. When I at last awoke, daylight was glancing across the foaming waters, the only sound I heard being that of their roar as they rushed over their rocky bed towards the valley below. I knelt down and prayed, as I had been accustomed to do from my childhood; and then, before resuming my journey, I took some of the scanty remains of the food I had brought with me, which I washed down with a draught from the stream.

Finding a practicable path to the left over the mountains, I followed it, still resolved not to trust myself in the neighbourhood of our foes. They could not have travelled over the mountains by night, but they might take it into their heads to follow me by day, and it would be unwise to linger. I did not slacken my speed, either, for if they did come they would move as fast as I could, and I might be overtaken. I stopped only occasionally, to eat a little food and to take a draught of water, of which I now found abundance by the way.

I cannot fully describe the events of that day. On and on I went, like a deer chased by the hunters. Sometimes I would fancy that I heard the war-whoops of the Indians behind me; at others the sounds which I conjured up appeared to be uttered by Bartle or Gideon. I would stop to listen, but only the roar of some distant waterfall or the murmur of a nearer rapid struck my ear. Or now and again I heard the cry of some bird of prey, as it swooped down from its lofty eyrie towards the carcass which it had espied far off on the plain below.

Again I was becoming faint with my exertions, and my food was exhausted. Whenever I stopped to rest, too, my mind dwelt upon the fearful scenes I had witnessed, and the fate of my friends. I was not altogether free from anxiety about Clarice, either. Brave and trustworthy as was my friend Manley, his party might have been pursued and overpowered by the savages, and my fair young sister might have been carried away into captivity, to suffer worse than death. To succumb, however, would have been unmanly. Although fatigued in body and anxious in mind, I had still sufficient physical strength to pursue my way.

The day was advancing, and I determined to strike down into the plains, where, at all events, I could make more rapid progress than over the rough ground I had been traversing. I accordingly directed my course, as I believed, to the eastward; but still hill beyond hill appeared, and it seemed as if I should never reach the more level ground. Still up and on I went, until at length I gained a height from whence, looking down, I saw that the prairie stretched out in the far distance before me.

I was descending at as rapid a rate as the ground would allow, when I caught sight, in the approaching gloom of evening, of the figure of a man. The person, whoever he was, had seen me as I appeared on the top of a rock exposed against the sky, and was coming towards me. To avoid him was impossible, so I got my weapons ready for an encounter, should he prove to be an enemy. Although he must have seen I held my rifle in my hand, he advanced without hesitation.

"What! do you not know me?" he exclaimed, when he got

nearer. "I am Winnemak, the friend of the Palefaces; although, alas! with but little power to assist them. You, however, I can aid, for I see you are weary and hungry. Come with me to where a few of my braves are encamped—but few, alas! the rest are killed or dispersed. We were on our way to the northward, where our squaws, children, and old men are encamped, when I caught sight of you as you came down the mountain, and I knew at once that you were flying from the Arrapahas."

This information explained Winnemak's unexpected appearance. Aided by him, I continued the descent of the mountain, although I believe without his support I could have gone no farther. He then told me all that had occurred.

Having visited Roaring Water and warned Uncle Jeff of the attack he knew would be made on the farm, he returned to where he had left his warriors, resolved to make a diversion in our favour, as he had promised. He had attacked the Arrapahas with much determination, but, overwhelmed by numbers, he had been driven back, with the loss of many of his followers. Having in vain attempted to reach the farm, he had stationed a band of his best warriors to afford us support should we have deserted the house, or attempted afterwards to cut our way out of it.

I was much disappointed to find that he could give me no information about Uncle Jeff, or about any of our friends; he was not even aware that Clarice had gone to join his daughter at the camp. He expressed his satisfaction at hearing that she had escaped the fate which had, he supposed, befallen all the inmates of the farm.

He now conducted me to his temporary camp, where we found a few of his warriors reclining on the ground. Several of them were wounded, and all looked weary and disheartened. They had, however, succeeded in killing a deer, and food was abundant. I was thankful to get a substantial meal, after which I lay down with the rest by the side of the stream, to obtain the sleep I so much needed.

A few skins had been stretched over some poles to afford shelter to the wounded, who required it more than the rest of us.

I had been asleep for several hours, when, suddenly awaking, I happened to turn my eyes across the stream, and saw, partly concealed by the brushwood, the figure of an Indian stooping down and apparently watching us. My first impulse was to jump up and present my rifle at him. I had, indeed, made some slight movement, when I felt a hand placed upon my arm. It was that of Winnemak.

"Hush!" he whispered. "I see the spy, and can kill him if I wish; but it is important to take him alive, to learn what he is about."

I observed, as he spoke, that he was freeing himself of such parts of his dress as might impede his progress, and that he was gradually creeping nearer and nearer to the edge of the stream. Being in the shade, he could not be seen by the stranger. Presently Winnemak rose to his feet, and making a spring, almost cleared the stream. With a few bounds he was on the opposite bank.

The spy saw him coming, and finding that he was discovered, rose from his recumbent position. He, too, was fleet of foot, and lightly clad. Away he rushed towards the level prairie; perhaps he expected to find friends there, or had his horse staked in that direction, near some wood or copse.

As soon as I perceived what Winnemak was about, I too sprang up, as did several Indians, but as they were all worn out with fatigue they were soon left behind. Being a good runner, I kept pace with the chief, although still at a considerable distance behind him, as he had had the start of me.

Day was just breaking, and there being no objects to impede the rays of the sun as it approached the horizon, the light rapidly increased. Although I had, at first, lost sight of Winnemak, I soon again saw him, with the man he was pursuing at no great distance in front.

On the two went. Neither of them being armed, the fight was not likely to be a bloody one; still it was evident that Winnemak attached great importance to the capture of the spy. Perhaps he suspected who he was; and he evidently entertained a bitter animosity against him. I could not have supposed that he would have exhibited so much activity, judging from his appearance when clothed in his usual robes. Although he appeared to be a strong, muscular man, the other Indian, from his movements, was evidently young and active. How he had ventured to approach the camp without being armed, was a mystery. He could not, at all events, have intended to injure any one, or he would have come with his bow and arrows. As the light rapidly increased, and I saw him more clearly than at first, it struck me that he was the young brave, Piomingo, who had lately paid us a visit at the farm; but of this, seeing him at the distance he was from me, I could not be certain.

The chase promised to be a far longer one than I had expected. The stranger seemed as resolved to escape as Winnemak was to overtake him. Few people, Indians or whites, except after long training, could have continued running so fast and for so long a period as did the spy and Winnemak.

I had the greatest difficulty in keeping near them; and, indeed, I had begun to fall behind, when I saw in front of me a broad piece of water. The fugitive saw it too, but had he turned either to the right or to the left it would have given an advantage to his pursuer; he therefore kept straight on.

His efforts to escape were vain. As he approached the bank the ground became so soft that his feet sunk deep into it at every step. He discovered, too late, his mistake. Springing back, he attempted to make his way to the right; but in doing so he fell. Recovering himself, however, he sprang back on to the firm ground; but seeing that escape by flight was no longer possible, he turned round and boldly faced his pursuer. At the same instant a wild swan, rising from the water, flew off with a loud cry. It might have been taken for the death-wail of one of the combatants. Like a couple of wild beasts, the two Indians rushed at each other, and the next instant they were clasped in a deadly embrace. A desperate struggle ensued. It was youth and activity opposed to well-knit muscles and firm nerves.

Fierce was the contest. The young man attempted to free himself from the grasp of his opponent; now they strove to seize each other by the throat; now his antagonist bore back the chief by making a desperate spring as his feet for a moment touched the ground; but if the older man allowed himself to retreat, it was only for the purpose of wearing out the strength of the younger, which he knew would soon be exhausted.

Winnemak now seized one of his antagonist's arms, and with a movement as quick as thought threw him on his back across his own knee; then pressing him down, it appeared to me that he intended to break his spine. A fearful shriek, wrung from him by the agony he was suffering, escaped the lips of the young brave; his eyes closed—the struggle was over. Still Winnemak did not let go his victim, but gazing fiercely down on his countenance until all appearance of life had ceased, he hurled the body to the ground. As he did so he exclaimed, "Stay there! You have betrayed me once; you would have stolen my daughter; you will no longer have the power to follow your evil practices."

The combat was over as I reached the place.

"Is he dead?" I asked, as I gazed down on the face of the vanquished brave.

"He will die," answered Winnemak; "but he still breathes."

"But I thought you wished to gain information from him?" I observed, feeling anxious to preserve the life of the poor wretch.

"I did; but now I would rather enjoy the pleasure of seeing him die."

"That is not the way we Palefaces treat a fallen enemy," I remarked. "You must not be displeased at what I say,—I would ask you to allow me to have him brought into the camp. At all events, for the present he can do no further harm, and he may wish to show his gratitude to those who have preserved his life."

"Do as you please," said the chief, after a moment's consideration.

I got some water from the lake,—finding a hard place by which I could approach it,—and threw it over the face of the fallen man, who had, I perceived, merely fainted from the excruciating pain he was suffering. He at length opened his eyes, and seemed to recognise me. It *was* Piomingo. The chief, I noticed, stood by, watching every movement of his late antagonist. I raised Piomingo's head, and was thankful to find that he now began to breathe more freely.

"Take care," said the chief. "He intends acting the part of the cunning fox, and will yet make an effort to escape."

Piomingo turned his eyes towards the speaker, apparently understanding him.

I was still making every effort to restore him, when several of Winnemak's followers came up.

"Then you grant my request?" I said, turning to the chief.

"I will not refuse you!" he answered; "but he will not thank you for the mercy you wish to show him."

I begged the Indians to assist me in carrying the injured man back to the camp, and the chief bade them do as I desired. Obtaining some poles from a copse which grew near, they quickly formed a litter, upon which they bore him back to the spot from which we had started. Not a groan escaped him, although I suspected, from the expression of his countenance, that he was suffering greatly. On arriving at the camp, in spite of my representations the chief ordered that his legs should be bound together, and that one of his hands should be fastened to a tree, so that he would be unable to escape.

Those who had remained in camp had prepared breakfast, to which even the wounded did ample justice. I took some food to the prisoner, who in a short time was able to swallow a little.

After some persuasion from me, and the promise of a

reward, four of the Indians undertook to carry their captive to the camp of Winnemak, to which we were bound; it was very evident that otherwise he must have been left to die miserably, as he was quite unable to walk. Three of the wounded men had also to be carried, so that we formed a mournful-looking party, as, shortly after our meal was finished, we commenced our march.

CHAPTER SEVEN

ON THE MARCH—WINNEMAK UNABLE TO GIVE ME NEWS OF MY FRIENDS—MY ARGUMENTS IN FAVOUR OF PIOMINGO—ENCAMPED FOR THE NIGHT—WE REACH WINNEMAK'S CAMP—BRAVES AND SQUAWS—WHERE ARE MY FRIENDS?—WINNEMAK AND HIS IDOLS—A PARTY OF BRAVES ARRIVE, WITH PRISONERS—MAYSOTTA AND HER DOG—A STRANGE MEETING—THE LIEUTENANT'S STORY—WE START IN QUEST OF CLARICE AND RACHEL—A FRUITLESS SEARCH—I LOSE MY FRIEND IN THE FOREST—TRYING TO REGAIN THE RIGHT PATH, I MEET WITH CLARICE AND MAYSOTTA—MY SISTER'S STORY—I TELL HER OF THE BURNING OF THE FARM—WE SET OUT FOR THE CAMP, AND MEET WITH THE LIEUTENANT—NIGHT COMING ON, WE ENCAMP IN THE FOREST—RESUMING OUR JOURNEY IN THE MORNING, WE REACH THE CAMP IN SAFETY.

As we proceeded on our journey, I walked alongside the chief, endeavouring to gain from him all the information I could. I was surprised that he had not fallen in with Uncle Jeff, and that he had seen nothing of Lieutenant Broadstreet and Clarice. I supposed that he or his people would certainly have met them on their way to his camp—Winnemak could only account for it by supposing that they had made a detour to avoid some party of the enemy.

"But might they not, then, have been surprised and overcome?" I asked, with much agitation.

"Not if they faced them with a bold front, or kept a proper watch at night," he answered. "Those Arrapahas are cowardly; they will only attack their enemies when they feel secure in their numbers, or can take them by surprise."

"They fought bravely enough when they assaulted Uncle Jeff's farm," I observed. "I should not have called them cowards."

"They had white men with them—and only the bravest of their warriors took part in the fight," he replied.

I could only trust that Winnemak was right in his conjecture, and that we should find Clarice and her escort at the camp. With regard to Uncle Jeff, I was still more anxious, and I began to fear that, notwithstanding his clever trick, he might not have escaped the bullets and arrows of his pursuers; or his horse might have fallen, and he have been taken prisoner. Altogether, my state of mind may be better imagined than described; still, always hopeful, I continued to hope, in spite of the appearance of things, that they would all turn up right at last.

I spoke to the chief on another subject. I was not altogether satisfied as to the way in which he intended to treat his prisoner, and he did not seem at all disposed to enlighten me. I told him how white men always fed their prisoners, and took good care of the wounded; and when war was over, set them free to return to their homes.

"The ways of the Palefaces are not those of the Redskins," he answered evasively. "Piomingo must be treated according to our customs; and my braves would complain were I to set him free to commit more mischief."

I pleaded for the poor wretch that he had not done us any injury as yet; that though he had been watching the camp, we could not tell that he had any sinister object in doing so; and that, as his life had been preserved, it would be barbarous to take it afterwards.

The chief heard me very patiently, but he was evidently unmoved by all my arguments.

I now and then went up and spoke to the poor prisoner, who, I suspected, was still suffering great pain, although Indian fortitude forbade him to give expression to his feelings. I urged his bearers, in the few words I could speak of their language, and by signs, to carry him carefully, for they were inclined to treat him as they would a deer or any other animal they might have shot. I saw the prisoner's eyes turned towards me, but he in no way expressed any gratitude for the service I desired to render him.

Winnemak was all this time keeping a look-out on every side; while several of his men were acting as scouts, so as to give us timely notice of danger.

At night we encamped as before, keeping a strict watch; while the prisoner was bound in a way which would have rendered it difficult for him to escape even had he possessed strength enough to run off. Our camp being pitched in a sheltered position, we lighted a fire, which even at that time of the year was pleasant, if not absolutely necessary; and there was but slight risk of its position betraying our presence to any passing foe.

The next morning we proceeded as before; and I was thankful when at length, just as evening was approaching, the chief told me that we were not far from the camp. I looked out eagerly ahead for the first sight of it, for I hoped to meet Clarice and Uncle Jeff there, and to have my anxiety at last set at rest.

The sun was just tinging the southern side of the snowy mountains on our left, ere it sank below them, when I caught sight of the wigwams of the Kaskaskias, on the slopes of a pine-covered hill. The camp as we drew near did not present a very attractive appearance. The wigwams were such as are only used in summer—a few poles, covered with buffalo hides, or deer skins, more to afford shelter from the heat of the sun, or from a downfall of rain, than protection from the cold. A number of squaws were seated about, some inside the tents nursing papooses, others tending large pots of broth boiling over fires. A few braves were standing about, and others looking after the horses of the tribe, which they had apparently just driven in from pasture; while a pack of dogs, the most ill-favoured of mongrels ever seen, were squatted about, watching for the offal which might be thrown to them, or ready to rush in and seize any of the meat which might for a moment be left unguarded.

The women continued at their various employments, but the braves, as we approached, advanced to meet us. The chief halted and addressed them, but I could not follow him. I judged, however, by the intonations of his voice, that he was telling them of his defeat, and the loss of so many of their people. Meantime, I was looking about eagerly for signs of Clarice, Uncle Jeff, and Manley, but nowhere could I see any. Still, I knew it would be contrary to Indian etiquette to interrupt the chief by inquiring for them.

On hearing of the various disasters which had occurred, the

men showed but little emotion. The chief, I observed, now pointed to his prisoner, by which I feared the worst for poor Piomingo.

As soon as I could venture to address the braves, I inquired for Clarice and the officer; and great was my dismay to find that they had not arrived at the camp, nor had Uncle Jeff appeared.

The chief now asked for his daughter.

Maysotta had gone out hunting with her favourite dog Keokuk. There was no danger of any harm befalling her while she had so good an attendant, as Keokuk knew when a foe was within a mile or so, and would give her ample warning; as he would were deer, buffalo, bears, or wolves within the same distance.

The chief, seeing my disappointment, endeavoured to console me by saying that perhaps my friends had missed the camp altogether, and had gone on, and that probably we should soon hear of them; a party of his braves were still out on an expedition, and they perhaps had fallen in with Clarice or Uncle Jeff.

No news was received during the night, but, in spite of my anxiety, I was glad to lie down in a corner of the chiefs tent and obtain some rest, of which I stood greatly in need. During our journey, when we might at any moment have been attacked by an enemy, I had only slept at intervals.

I had been for some hours, I fancy, fast asleep, when I was awakened by a movement made by the chief, who had been lying near by me, wrapped in his buffalo robe. By the light of the moon, which streamed in through the unclosed entrance, I saw him get up and leave the tent.

Influenced by a motive for which I cannot now account, I rose and followed him. My belief is that I was scarcely awake; indeed, I walked along like a person in a dream. He at once left the camp, and took the way down to the lower and open ground. I was at some distance behind him, so he did not hear my footsteps.

After walking for a quarter of an hour or more, I found myself in the midst of an Indian burial-ground, which I recognised by the number of small platforms, raised on posts and thatched over, rising in all directions. Besides the platforms, I observed several strange-looking figures fixed to the top of tall poles, and composed, as far as I could judge, of bits of coloured rags and skins, which fluttered in a weird fashion in the night breeze.

The chief stopped before a couple of these fantastic-looking objects, and, with folded arms, gazed up at them, uttering some words which I was too far off to hear distinctly, though the sound of his voice reached my ears. He was praying,—of that I could have no doubt,—and these trumpery scarecrows were his idols. I could not have supposed that a man of good sense, as he appeared to be, could be the victim of a superstition so gross and contemptible.

He continued standing for some time, making various signs, and uttering words as before.

Unwilling to be discovered, now that I was fully awake, I was on the point of retreating, when the sound of my footfall reached his ears, and turning round he saw me. I did not wish that he should fancy I was afraid of encountering him, so I at once advanced, and told him frankly how I came to follow him. I assured him, also, that I had had no intention of acting as a spy on his movements. As he appeared to be in no way displeased, I asked him, while we were walking back to the camp, whether he had really been worshipping the figures I had seen.

"Why not?" he inquired in a serious tone. "The times are full of danger and difficulty, and I wished to obtain the protection and support of the guardian spirits of our people. If I did not ask them, how could I expect them to grant me what I want? While I was staying at Roaring Water, I heard your uncle pray to your gods; and I suppose that you expected them to give you what you asked for."

I tried to explain to him that there is but one God, the Great Spirit of whom his people knew, though they were sadly ignorant of his character; and that we never prayed to inferior beings, as our God would not allow us to do so. Much more I said, though at the time with little effect; indeed, the chief was as deeply sunk in the grossest superstition as are the Indian tribes among whom the gospel light has not yet shone.

On reaching his tent, he bade me lie down again, observing that he would talk over the matter another day.

The next morning I was surprised to find that Maysotta had not returned. Still, her father appeared to feel no anxiety about her.

The sun had been up a couple of hours or so when I heard shouts in the camp, and the chief with all his braves hurried out. They went to welcome the return of a party of their warriors, who marched in singing and shouting,—the leading men having three or four scalps at the end of their spears, while among them were dragged three or four unfortunate Arrapahas, whom they had captured, and who were, according to the Indian custom, to be put to death. Among them, to my surprise and horror, was a young squaw, who, if not beautiful according to my taste, was certainly interesting-looking. She bore herself with as much fortitude, apparently, as the men, although she knew that her fate would be the same as theirs.

The chief had said nothing to me about Piomingo, and I now felt satisfied that it was the intention of his people to sacrifice him with the rest of the prisoners. I resolved, however, to plead for him, as well as for them, and make special endeavours to save the life of the young squaw. According to the savage Indian custom, she would be barbarously tortured before being put to death. It seems strange that human beings can take a pleasure in thus treating their fellow-creatures; it shows how debased, how diabolically cruel, men can become when they have once gone away from God. At present, however, the braves were too much occupied in recounting their deeds of valour to think of their prisoners, who were left bound, and guarded with lynx-eyed watchfulness by some of the old squaws.

I found that this was only one of the parties of braves, and that another was expected shortly with more prisoners. As far as I could understand, these prisoners were said to be white men; but I concluded that they were some of the Mexican outlaws who had accompanied the Arrapahas on their marauding expedition.

While looking out for them, I saw a solitary figure, rifle in hand, approaching the camp, whom I recognised as Maysotta, accompanied by her dog Keokuk. I hastened to meet her, and told her of my anxiety at the non-appearance of Clarice.

"If they do not come, I will go in search of them," she said.

She had killed a deer, so she sent off some of her people,

under the guidance of Keokuk, to bring it in. Her dog would, she said, lead them to the spot.

Shortly afterwards, the second band, who were expected, made their appearance in the distance, and, as before, the warriors hurried out to meet them.

I was still talking to Maysotta, when I saw her look towards the approaching party, and an expression of astonishment take possession of her countenance.

"What have our braves been doing?" she said. "They have made a prisoner of our friend the young white chief."

As she spoke, I looked in the same direction, and I too was greatly astonished, and also much alarmed, at seeing Lieutenant Broadstreet, with his arms tied behind him, in the midst of the warriors—his two troopers following, closely guarded.

"What can have happened?" I exclaimed. "What can have become of Clarice and Rachel? My dear sister! some accident must have befallen her."

"I will learn what has happened," said Maysotta.

I hurried to Winnemak, and explained that his people had made prisoners of those who were on their way to visit his camp.

He thought I was mistaken; but I assured him that I was not, and that his daughter would corroborate my statement. On hearing this he ordered the prisoners to be brought forward, when, at once recognising the lieutenant and the two troopers, he ordered them to be set at liberty.

Hurrying up to my friend, I eagerly inquired for Clarice and her attendant.

His emotion would scarcely allow him to reply. He seemed dreadfully cast down, as well as weak and faint from want of food.

"We had encamped two nights ago," he said, "in a secure spot, as I supposed, and were in hopes the next day of reaching our destination, when just at dusk I saw a band of Indians approaching. To prevent them coming near, I ordered my men to mount and ride forward, while your sister and Rachel remained, as I hoped, concealed from view. The Indians retreated to some distance, and I was induced to follow. They then halted and made signs of friendship, which tempted me to go still nearer. Suddenly, however, as I was about to inquire who they were, and where they were going, they set upon me and my men, without the slightest warning, and before we could even draw our swords or pistols we were dragged from our horses, and our arms bound behind us. At first I thought that our captors must be Arrapahas; but looking again at their costume, I was sure that they were Kaskaskias, belonging to a friendly tribe. In vain I expostulated, and tried to explain who we were; but they did not understand me, mistaking us, I believe, for some of the Mexicans who had accompanied the Arrapahas; at all events, we were dragged ignominiously along, neither food nor water being given us."

I at once told the chief what the lieutenant had said. He was very indignant with his people, but explained that the whole had happened by mistake.

Our first thought, of course, was to discover Clarice and Rachel. The lieutenant himself was eager to start immediately, but he was evidently too weak for the undertaking, and was at once led to the chief's tent, where Maysotta hurried to attend on him, while some of the older squaws took care of his two troopers.

Maysotta immediately brought him food and water. "Eat," she said; "the 'Fair Lily' is my friend as well as yours; I am as anxious as you are to find her. As soon as you are rested we will set out. Were you to go now, you would faint by the way."

I was standing outside the entrance to the tent while Maysotta was speaking to the lieutenant, and it struck me, from her looks and tone of voice, that she felt a warm interest in the young lieutenant, which might, I feared, prove inconvenient, if it had not worse consequences.

I was watching the Indians, who, having lost their white prisoners, had now brought forward their Redskin captives, and were dancing a horrible war-dance round them. Their appearance on ordinary occasions was somewhat savage, but they looked ten times more savage now, as they shrieked, and leaped, and tossed their arms and legs about, and went round and round, flourishing their tomahawks, and jeering at the unfortunate people in their midst. The latter, knowing that they would not yet be sacrificed, sat in perfect silence, without exhibiting any emotion, and bearing patiently the insults heaped upon them.

I had not abandoned my idea of pleading for the unhappy prisoners, but at this time I was thinking more of Clarice, and the means of recovering her; still, should I go away, I feared that the prisoners might be put to death during my absence. Having seen that the horses of my white friends were turned out on a pasture close at hand, where they could get abundance of grass, I went to the chief and asked him whether he wished to be on friendly terms with the Palefaces?

He said that he certainly did—it was his greatest ambition.

"Then," I replied, "you must live as they do, and imitate their customs. I have told you before, that we do not torture or otherwise injure our prisoners, and that it is our duty to forgive our enemies, and to do them good. Now I want you to promise me that no one shall suffer while I am away."

The chief could not make up his mind to yield, but I urged him again and again, and at last I hoped, from what he said, that he would do as I wished.

The lieutenant was now sufficiently recovered to mount his horse, and, followed by his two troopers, he and I set off in search of Clarice. None of the Indians, however, offered to accompany us, nor did Maysotta, as I thought she would have done; but I found that she had left the camp with her dog and rifle before we started. It was her custom, I discovered, to act in a very independent manner on all occasions, her father never interfering with her.

We pushed forward at as rapid a rate as we could make our horses move; but the ground was at first too rough to allow us to proceed as fast as we wished. When we got to the plain we gave our steeds the rein.

Judging from the report of Winnemak's people who last came in, we had not much risk of encountering any of our foes; indeed, our whole thoughts were entirely occupied by Clarice and Rachel. Had they waited quietly the return of their escort; or had any hostile Indians discovered them, and carried them off as captives? The idea of such an occurrence as that was too horrible to be contemplated. Perhaps they might have caught and mounted their horses, and set off to try and find their way to the camp. In that case we might possibly meet them, and as we rode along we kept a strict look-out on every side.

"Can they possibly have passed us?" I inquired of my companions.

"I do not see how that can be, unless they should have gone very much out of their way; and I remember having pointed out to your sister the position of the Indian camp, so that she would know how to direct her course," answered Manley. "The peculiar form of the mountains above it would be sufficient to guide her."

After all, we felt that there was but little use in talking about the matter, or in surmising what might have happened—though, of course, we did talk on without ceasing.

We at last approached the spot where Manley had left Clarice and her companion. Should we not find them there, we must endeavour to follow their trail; and when I thought of the possibility of having to do this, I regretted not having endeavoured to induce an Indian to accompany us.

"There is the place," said Manley, at length; "but I see no smoke, and had they remained they would certainly have kept up a fire."

We rode forward eagerly; but our fears were realised. The ashes of the fire at the camp were there, but the fire itself had long been extinguished.

Clarice and Rachel must have left the spot some time before!

We searched about in every direction, but could find no traces of their having been there lately, and our eyes were not sufficiently sharp to distinguish the signs which would have enabled an Indian to say in what direction they had gone. We next looked out for their horses, but they were nowhere within sight.

Some time was thus spent, and the day was drawing to a close. Should we not find them before nightfall, we must wait until the next morning. To have to do this was trying in the extreme, but we had to submit, as it was so dark that we could with difficulty see our way as we returned to the deserted camp. My poor friend Manley was dreadfully out of spirits, but I assured him that he had no reason to blame himself. He had acted for the best, and no man could do more.

The next morning we resumed our search; but without success. We were both of us in despair.

"They must have taken their horses and ridden off towards the mountains; it is useless searching for them here any longer," I said.

Manley agreed with me, and, believing that they must have gone on to the camp by a different route from the one we had taken, he was eager to return.

He and his men had pushed ahead through the forest while I stopped to tighten the girths of my saddle; and when I rode forward, expecting immediately to overtake them, I found that I had followed a different direction from that which they had taken.

It is no easy matter, in a thick forest, to regain the right path, or to get up with those who have once been lost sight of. I found it to be so in the present instance. I was sure that I could not be going very far wrong, and expected as soon as I reached the edge of the forest to see my friends, although they might have got some little way ahead on the open ground.

As I was riding on, I fancied that I heard the bark of a dog. I listened, and again heard the same sound. I was now certain that the animal was not far off. To whom could it belong? The dog was not likely to be wandering by itself in the forest. I rode in the direction from whence the sound proceeded, and in a short time reached a somewhat more open part of the forest. Great was my surprise and joy to see my dear little sister Clarice, leaning on the arm of Maysotta, who carried her rifle in her hand, while Keokuk ran beside her.

Leaping from my horse, I sprang towards Clarice, who threw her arms round my neck, exclaiming, "O Ralph, I am so thankful to see you! I have been in a dreadful state of alarm and anxiety, thinking that Manley—I mean Lieutenant Broadstreet—and his men had been killed. Maysotta has somewhat relieved my mind. But where is he? Has he been unable to come and look for me?"

The assurance I gave that Manley was well, and not far off, soon restored Clarice to her usual composure.

Having no longer any fears about Manley's safety, she was able to answer the questions I put to her. After telling me how the lieutenant and his men had ridden off to meet the Indians, she continued:—

"We were sitting before the fire awaiting their return, when what was our dismay to see two huge wolves approaching the camp, followed by a number of cubs! Our first impulse was to fly; and while the wolves stopped to eat up our provisions, we were able to escape to a distance. We took refuge in the hollow of a tree, which afforded us sufficient shelter, and the aperture being some way up, we felt sure the wolves could not make their way in. But Maysotta has been telling me that something dreadful has happened, though I cannot make out what she means."

"I will tell you all about that by-and-by," I answered; "but I am eager to know how Maysotta managed to find you."

"As soon as we thought that the wolves had gone from our camp, Rachel went to see if anything had been left; but the savage creatures had carried off everything, and at the same time frightened away our horses and mules, and they were nowhere to be seen. We remained in the tree for some time, and I do not think anybody would have found us. Then Rachel went away to try and get some berries and roots. She had not been long absent when I heard a dog barking, and looking out through a small hole in the hollow trunk, I saw Maysotta approaching. I therefore stepped out of my place of concealment; and Maysotta, who was delighted to find me, said that she had come out expressly to search for us, and would take us immediately to the camp. Of course, I could not go without Rachel, and we are now on our way to look for her, as she cannot be far off."

"Keokuk will find her," said Maysotta, patting her dog on the head, and saying a few words to him.

Away he started, and in a short time we heard him barking loudly. Maysotta, leaving Clarice with me, hurried on, and in a few minutes we saw her approach, guiding Rachel towards us.

Rachel's joy on seeing me was so demonstrative, that I scarcely liked to tell her or my sister of the destruction of the farm. However, it had to be done, and I related all that had taken place. As I proceeded, Rachel gave full vent to her grief, whilst my sister betrayed the sorrow she felt by her tearful and troubled countenance. Rachel wrung her hands and burst into tears, which her own previous perilous position had not been able to draw from her.

"De farm burned!" she exclaimed; "oh dear! oh dear! And what become of Jenny, Nancy, Polly, and all de oder cows, and de pigs and de poultry? And Uncle Jeff, what he do; and Bartle and Gideon?"

I consoled her somewhat by saying that I thought it possible all three had escaped, and that even the cows and pigs might have got away, either into the woods or among the hills.

On hearing this she became somewhat more tranquil, and was able to chat away in her usual style.

We now prepared to set out for the camp. I thought it probable, on account of the delay, that we might not overtake Manley, although I specially wished to do so, in order to put an end to his anxiety. It was, of course, important to recover the horses and baggage-mules, and Maysotta proposed that she should conduct us to the edge of the forest, where we could remain while she, with Keokuk, searched for the animals,—expressing, at the same time, her confidence of success.

Having placed Clarice on my horse, I led the animal by the rein till we reached the spot proposed. We looked out to the westward for Manley and his troopers, and were greatly disappointed at not seeing them. So, I suspect, was Clarice. We had not, however, waited long until I caught sight of three horsemen. They came rapidly on, and to my great satisfaction I distinguished our friends. On observing us they put spurs to their horses, and the lieutenant galloped forward.

Clarice met him with a sweet smile.

"I felt very sure that you had not willingly deserted us," she answered, when, in an agitated voice, Manley told her of the anguish of his mind at finding himself a prisoner in the hands of the Indians, leaving her unprotected in the forest.

As we could not tell how long Maysotta might be absent, we lighted a fire and cooked some provisions, of which both Clarice and Rachel stood greatly in need. The Indian damsel, however, had been so confident about finding the horses, that I was not surprised to see Keokuk driving them towards us, a short time before sunset.

Maysotta expressed her satisfaction at finding the young white chief, as she called Manley, and his men with us. "As it is now too late to set off to-night," she said, "we must remain here. There are water and grass near at hand; and if your men will do as I direct them, we will quickly put up a wigwam for Clarice, the black woman, and me."

Manley and I offered to act under her directions; but, except that we cut some rough sticks, and transported some bark, she really gave us very little to do,—performing nearly the whole of the architectural operations with her own hands.

I was thankful that Clarice would thus have shelter, and be able to obtain the rest which she so much required.

Maysotta had shot several small animals, and these, with the provisions we had brought, afforded us an abundant supper.

The night was passed without any interruption, and early the next morning we set off for Winnemak's camp. I offered to take Maysotta on my horse, but she declined, saying that she would proceed on foot, as she hoped to shoot some deer by the way.

We rode as fast as we could; indeed, I was most anxious to

get back, both on account of the unhappy captives, and because I hoped to hear news of Uncle Jeff.

As we got into the neighbourhood of the camp, we caught sight, on the summit of a slight elevation, of a single horseman, who sat his steed without moving, apparently unable to make out who we were, as, lifting his hand to his brow, he peered at us from under it. We had got within speaking distance before I recognised our host Winnemak. His whole appearance and bearing were totally changed. With a magnificent crown of feathers on his head, a jacket of rich fur handsomely trimmed, glittering bracelets and earrings, a spear in his hand and a shield at his back, as he firmly sat his strongly-built mustang, he looked every inch a warrior chief.

"I did not know you at first, but I do now," he said, smiling; "and the White Lily is truly welcome to my tents."

Clarice thanked him, and we rode to the camp together. He told us that he purposed visiting the chiefs of all the neighbouring tribes and forming a confederation, in order to resist effectually any future invasion of our common enemies the Arrapahas. "For such a purpose a chief must be habited as becomes a chief," he added, to account to us for the change in his costume.

I scarcely listened to him, however, as I was eagerly waiting to inquire if Uncle Jeff had arrived at the camp; and I was much disappointed to find that nothing had been seen or heard of him.

CHAPTER EIGHT

I SEEK OUT PIOMINGO—A STRONG DESIRE TO SAVE HIS LIFE—I PLEAD WITH THE CHIEF, AND GAIN MY POINT—I OFFER THE YOUNG BRAVE MY HORSE AND ARMS—KINDNESS REQUITED—THE INDIAN'S ESCAPE—A DARING ACT, AND A KIND DEED—WE SEEK PROTECTION FROM THE INDIANS—RETURN OF UNCLE JEFF AND MAYSOTTA—AN ADDRESS TO THE BRAVES—HOW IT SUCCEEDED—UNCLE JEFF'S STORY—THE LIEUTENANT ABOUT TO LEAVE US—HIS PLANS—WE SEND OUT SCOUTS—ALARMING INTELLIGENCE—THE CAMP STRUCK—WE MOVE TO THE NORTHWARD—WE CHANGE OUR PLANS—A WONDERFUL REGION—WE SEPARATE FROM OUR INDIAN FRIENDS—THROUGH A PINE FOREST—THE CATARACT OF THE PASS—WE SEND BACK OUR HORSES—OUR JOURNEY CONTINUED—A "CANADA STAG" KILLED—ENCAMPED FOR THE NIGHT.

The chief, who seemed inclined to treat us with every kindness, immediately ordered a wigwam to be put up for Clarice and Rachel, and another for Manley and me.

In the meantime, feeling interested in the fate of Piomingo, I went to seek him out. I found him lying on the ground, under the shade of some trees, to one of which he was secured by ropes. I asked him if he desired to escape.

"Yes," he replied; "life is sweet. But I am prepared to die as becomes a brave, if my enemies are resolved to take my life."

"If you were free, what would you do?" I asked.

"I would endeavour to rescue the young squaw who was brought in a prisoner two days ago; she is the maiden I was about to make my wife. Life without her would be of little value to me; were she to be put to death, I should be ready to die with her."

"But are you able to move?" I asked.

"The pain has left my back, and I am as strong as ever," he answered. "Give me the opportunity, and you will see how I shall act."

Feeling a strong desire to save the lives of these two young people at every risk, I immediately went back to the chief, and used every argument in my power to induce him to set Piomingo at liberty. I pointed out to him how it was far more noble to forgive an injury than to avenge it, and that if he allowed Piomingo to go free he would make him his friend for life.

"If you choose to set him at liberty, you are welcome to do so," he said at last; "but he is unable to move, and if he remains in this camp he will be killed."

"I will see to that, and assist him to get away," I answered.

I hurried back to where Piomingo lay, and at once undid the cords which bound him.

"I feel that my strength has returned, and that I shall be able to perform whatever I undertake," he said.

"I do not wish to do things by halves," I remarked. "You shall have my horse; I will place the animal in yonder wood. If you have an opportunity, you can return him; but if not, I will give him to you."

"Young Paleface," he said, struck by my kindness, "Piomingo would wish to serve you for the remainder of his days; perhaps he will have an opportunity of showing his gratitude; but he would ask you to show him your generosity still further. Supply him with arms; without them, he may fall a victim to the first foe he meets."

"I will give you my knife and sword, but you must promise me not to use them against any of the people of this tribe except in self-defence, should they attempt to recapture you."

Piomingo swore by the Great Spirit that he would act as I desired.

"I will leave the sword and knife close to the tree to which I will secure my horse," I said on leaving him.

I thought it better not to question him as to his intentions in regard to the young squaw, although I had my suspicions on the subject.

I forthwith went for my horse, which I led to the wood, as I had promised. All the Indians were so much engaged that they took no notice of my proceedings; and when every arrangement had been made, I returned to Piomingo.

Grasping my hand, he exclaimed,—"You are more generous than I deserve; for when I went to your farm it was with the intention of working you evil. But after I saw the 'Fair Lily,' your sister, I had not the heart to do her an injury; and instead of remaining and opening the gate to your enemies, as I had intended, I made my escape. When I was watching your camp, it was with no treacherous design. I wished to warn you that the Arrapahas were still advancing, and that their purpose was to occupy the passes through the mountains, so that they could intercept you and any other Palefaces who might travel in that direction. They must, by this time, have carried out that part of their plan, so that I would advise you and your friends to pass on more to the north, by which means you may escape them. I have also to tell you that one of your people is in their hands. They have been carrying him about with them from place to place; but whether they intend to kill him, as they have done the other prisoners, I could not learn."

I thanked Piomingo for his information, which, I felt sure, gratitude had prompted him to give. And, of course, I resolved to urge the chief to act upon it.

On questioning Piomingo, I was convinced, from the description he gave of the white man who had been made prisoner, that it must be either Gideon or Bartle. I had great hopes, at all events, that Uncle Jeff had escaped from his pursuers; but what had since become of him I could not conjecture, nor could Piomingo give me any information.

It was now sufficiently dark to allow of the captive making his escape without being observed. I again cast off the ropes, therefore, and stole quietly away from the spot. The moment I had gone, he must have crept away—crouching down, Indian fashion, until he had got to a safe distance from the camp, when, having first secured the weapons I had left for him, he must have mounted my horse and galloped off.

The next day had been fixed for the death of the prisoners, so I boldly told the chief that, taking advantage of his permission, I had set Piomingo at liberty, and urged him to be equally generous towards the young squaw.

"My people will complain if they are disappointed," he answered, turning aside.

I was sorry that I could not see Maysotta, as she might have effectually pleaded for one of her own sex.

Stakes had now been driven into the ground, and every preparation made for the horrible sacrifice. But, looking at the captives, I should not have supposed that they were to be the victims. Even the young squaw retained her composure.

I spoke to Manley on the subject. "We must not allow these savages to carry out their cruel intention," I said. "If you and your men will assist, we might set them free."

"I would gladly do as you propose," he answered, "but it would be at the sacrifice, probably, of our own lives and that of your sister. These Redskins now treat us with every respect; but were we to interfere with their customs, they would naturally turn upon us."

I felt that he was right in that respect; but still I could not bear the thought of allowing the horrible deed to be perpetrated, without again interceding for the victims.

The hour now approached for the death of the prisoners, and finding that Piomingo had escaped, the Redskins were the more eager to put to death those who remained in their power. They were therefore led out and bound to the stakes, and the savages commenced their horrible war-dance round them.

Manley and I again pleaded with the chief.

"It is useless," answered Winnemak; "I have said it, and it must be done."

Just then, from behind the shelter of a wood on one side of the mountains, a mounted warrior dashed out. I saw at once that it was Piomingo. His eyes were fixed on one point; it was the spot where the young squaw was bound. Quick as lightning he cut the cords which bound her, and placing her before him on the saddle, galloped off, and was out of reach before those at hand could hinder him. Fortunately, none of Winnemak's people had firearms, and their bows and arrows having been laid aside, they hurried to their wigwams to obtain them. But ere bow could be drawn the rescued squaw and her deliverer were far beyond their reach. In vain were showers of arrows sent after them; the fugitives heeded them not. Many of the braves ran for their horses; but I well knew that my gallant steed, even with two people on his back, could keep ahead of them.

The whole camp was soon in confusion and astonishment at the audacity of the act. Some of the braves may have suspected that I had had a hand in the business, for I observed that they cast angry glances at me as they passed. So great was their excitement, too, that for the moment they had forgotten the other prisoners.

Just then I met Sergeant Custis and Pat Sperry.

"Now is our time to do a kind deed," I said; "it may be at some risk, but let us set the other prisoners free."

"Sure, won't I, thin!" cried Pat.

"I will venture on it," said the sergeant.

We hurried to the spot, and, in spite of the expostulations of a few old squaws who had remained to watch them, we cut the ropes which bound the unhappy captives to the stakes.

"Now run for your lives!" I exclaimed.

The released prisoners did not require a second bidding, although the old squaws tried to stop them. They were all young and active men, too, and before any of the braves had returned from their futile chase after Piomingo, the fugitives had got to a considerable distance from the camp.

As I knew that our part in the affair must at once become known, I immediately hastened to the chief.

"I have saved you from committing a great crime, which would have made you despised and hated by all white men," I exclaimed, with a boldness at which I myself was surprised. "If my uncle were here he would speak as I do, and approve of my conduct."

The chief appeared to be dumbfounded at my audacity; but, although he himself would not have interfered, I do not think he was really sorry that the prisoners had escaped.

"I must get you to protect us from your people when they return," I said. "We have no wish to take the places of the prisoners, or to have bloodshed in the matter. At the same time, we are resolved to fight for our lives, should your people attempt to molest us."

"You indeed speak boldly," said the chief. "But I will

endeavour to prevent further mischief, and will tell my people all you have said."

Almost immediately afterwards the braves came hurrying back to the camp, when the old squaws commenced in screeching tones to tell them what had occurred. The warriors on this advanced towards us with threatening looks. The chief stepped forward, and holding up his hands, they at once stopped and prepared to listen to him. He possibly may have made a very eloquent speech in our favour, but his braves were evidently not satisfied. We saw them making violent gestures, and, from the words which reached us, I made out that they insisted on our being delivered up to suffer in the place of the prisoners we had liberated.

Lieutenant Broadstreet, who had now joined us, rifle in hand, told me to say to the chief that if his people were injured an army of white men would be sent by his Government against them, and not one would be allowed to escape.

Although, I believe, the chief spoke as I begged him, the angry braves were not to be appeased, still crying out that we must be handed over to them.

"Not while we have got a cartridge left in our pouches," cried Sergeant Custis, lifting his rifle as he spoke, as if he intended to make use of it, while Manley, Pat, and I followed his example.

Just at this juncture two persons were seen approaching the camp,—the one was Maysotta, accompanied by Keokuk, the other was a tall person dressed in skins. At first I did not recognise him; but on looking again, what was my joy to see Uncle Jeff! Both he and Maysotta must have observed that something unusual was taking place in the camp, for they hurried forward at a quick pace, and in another moment had approached the chief.

Uncle Jeff at once put out his hand. "What does all this mean?" he asked.

Winnemak was silent.

"I will tell you all about it, Uncle Jeff," I said; and I briefly related what had occurred.

"You acted rightly, Ralph," he answered. "It would never do for white men to stand by and see murder committed, which proper boldness could prevent. Hand me a few cartridges, for I have expended my ammunition; and although we are five to fifty, I feel very sure these fellows will not interfere with us. However, we will try fair means first; and the young squaw will, I am sure, be on our side."

He at once turned to Maysotta, and telling her what had occurred, begged her to plead with her father and his people. She did not seem to think it necessary to say anything to Winnemak, but at once addressed herself to the braves, over whom it was evident she had great influence.

I saw the angry expression gradually disappear from their countenances; their gestures became less menacing, and at length their fury completely subsided. Maysotta saw the advantage she had gained, and went on to tell them that we were their guests, and that, even had we been guilty of a greater provocation, they were bound to protect our lives with their own; that we had always been friendly with the red men; and, above all, that we had preserved the life of their chief, who, had it not been for us, would have died. She by this means completely won over the braves, but she had a harder task with the old squaws. Finally, however, she succeeded with them, and what appeared at one time to threaten a serious termination was at length settled to the satisfaction of all parties.

We promised, as soon as we could obtain them, presents of tobacco, blankets, and beads for the squaws, and some arms and ammunition for the braves, on condition that they would always use them in our service.

We were, of course, very eager to hear how Uncle Jeff had escaped. I noticed, besides, that he looked fatigued and careworn, and had evidently suffered much.

"I had a narrow escape from my pursuers, on leaving the farm," he said, "for more than one bullet whistled close to my ears, while two entered the sides of my brave Jack—who bore me, notwithstanding, for many a mile, until I had left my enemies far behind. Then my gallant steed sank down and died. As I was making my way northward on foot, I caught sight of several parties of Arrapahas. This made me feel very anxious on account of Clarice and her escort, who, I feared, might have fallen into their hands. I myself had some difficulty in avoiding them, and at length I found it necessary to take to the mountains, where, at the same time, I should have a better chance of killing game. Unfortunately, for the first time in my life I became very ill, and had to remain for several days in a cave, hardly able to crawl out and get a draught of water from a spring hard by. Recovering, I moved on again; but having exhausted the few cartridges I possessed, I was reduced to hard straits for food.

"I was making my way on when I heard a shot fired; and as I approached the spot, I saw a young Indian girl who had just killed a small deer. Her quick eye caught sight of me at the same moment. I made signs to her that I was desperately hungry, and she in turn pointed to the deer; so, as she appeared in no way alarmed at seeing me, I at once went up to her. After exchanging a few words, it occurred to me that she must be the daughter of our friend Winnemak; and on my asking her, she said that such was the case. I then informed her who I was; upon which she immediately cut up the deer, lighted a fire, and prepared such a meal as I had not enjoyed for many a day. I soon felt my strength wonderfully restored, and my spirits rose when she told me that Clarice and you were safe. We accordingly at once set off for the camp, and I am thankful that we arrived in time to settle matters amicably with our friends here."

The arrival of Uncle Jeff produced a great improvement in the state of affairs. The Indians had all heard of him, and Winnemak treated him with the greatest respect. Uncle Jeff was indeed likely to exercise a beneficial influence over the tribe. He told them that although men had a right to defend themselves against their enemies, the Great Spirit disliked their making war one upon another; that he wished them all to live at peace with their fellow-creatures; to provide proper food, clothing, and shelter for their squaws and papooses; and that the Great Spirit intended that they should cultivate the ground, and not depend upon the precarious supply which the chase afforded. Uncle Jeff told them also that the Great Spirit loved them all, and wished them to be his children; that they were very wicked, but that he was ready to forgive them, and had sent One on earth, his own dear Son, who had consented to be punished instead of them, that he might become their Elder Brother, and that they might enjoy the affection and privileges bestowed by the Father upon his children.

Uncle Jeff was not much of a preacher, but, as he said, he might manage to break ground, so that any missionary coming after him would be more likely to be well received.

Clarice did not fail to talk to Maysotta on the same subject;

and the Indian girl appeared to take in the truths of the gospel much more readily than did the men of her tribe.

* * * * *

Although the camp was pitched in a tolerably secure position, both Uncle Jeff and Winnemak considered it necessary to send out scouts in order to ascertain what the enemy were about.

Lieutenant Broadstreet, who had no longer any excuse for remaining with us, felt that it was his duty to proceed, with the two troopers, on his journey. But he was evidently very unwilling to leave Clarice; and I suspect that she also had no wish to let him go.

"I cannot tell to what dangers you may be exposed, and I shall be in a miserable state of anxiety until I once more have the happiness of seeing you," he said to her. "My intention is to point out the state of affairs to the commandant at Fort Harwood, and induce him to obtain such a body of troops as will effectually overawe the savages and drive them back to the southward, so that your uncle and other settlers may be able to resume possession of their property, and for the future live in peace. The sooner, therefore, I set out, the more quickly will this desirable object be attained."

"I highly applaud your intention, lieutenant," said Uncle Jeff; "and I speak honestly when I say that, if you wish at any time to turn your sword into a ploughshare, as the saying is, I shall be happy to have you for a neighbour; and come when you may, you shall always be welcome at Roaring Water. I hope that it will not be long before I am back there again. I only wish I knew what has become of Bartle and Gideon; if they are alive, we shall very soon get the farm built up again, and everything put to rights."

The first of the scouts who had been sent out soon came back, with the information that the enemy were still in considerable numbers in the neighbourhood. Winnemak and Uncle Jeff agreed, therefore, that it would be prudent to move further to the north, in consequence of what Piomingo had told me. Camp was accordingly struck, and the baggage animals—which, I am sorry to say, for the sake of my Redskin friends, included a number of the squaws—were loaded. A small party of warriors going ahead acted as an advance-guard, while the remainder of the tribe brought up the rear, or went as scouts on either hand.

As the lieutenant had to follow the same road for some distance, we continued together,—he, as may be supposed, riding alongside of Clarice. I do not know what Uncle Jeff thought about the matter, but it was evident to me that Clarice and Manley were very fond of one another. However, as I thought highly of him, I did not feel myself called upon to interfere in the matter.

We had proceeded some distance, when another of the scouts came in with the alarming intelligence that the enemy, in considerable numbers, were ahead of us, and that it was too probable they intended to attack us on our march. We had therefore to proceed with greater caution than before; and the advance-guard was considerably strengthened, so that they might be able to keep an enemy in check until the remainder of the tribe could come up.

It was too evident that the Arrapahas had overrun the country, and that it would be some time before they could be expelled; and, such being the case, Uncle Jeff said he would fix upon another location, perhaps to the west of the Rocky Mountains, where the Indians were friendly, and where he would still be near enough to the high-road to obtain a market for his produce.

He had, consequently, just settled to accompany the lieutenant through the pass, when another scout came in with the information that the Arrapahas had taken possession of the pass itself, and that they had so fortified themselves that they could not be driven out except by a strong party, and at considerable loss of life.

This made it necessary for Uncle Jeff and Manley to change their plans. They settled that we should proceed northwards with the Indians, while they reconnoitred the pass; promising, should they find the account they had received to be correct, to rejoin us, and perhaps attempt to cross the mountains so as to reach the western plains. The mountains to the northwards, however, were but little known, and even Winnemak confessed that he had never wandered among them. He had heard, he said, that there was a wonderful region in that direction, where the earth trembled frequently; the fountains, instead of being cold, were hot, and that the water was seen rushing upwards in huge jets; and that there were lakes amid the mountains, and torrents, and waterfalls such as were nowhere else to be seen.

"If the chiefs account is correct, it must be an interesting region to visit," said Sergeant Custis. "For my own part, I hope we shall have the chance of getting there."

While travelling on we kept in compact order, looking out, as usual, for the approach of foes; but happily none appeared. Crossing the road which led to the pass, we continued onwards until nightfall. We then encamped in as strong a position as we could find. We knew it was of no use to attempt concealing the route we had followed; for even had we taken the greatest pains to do so, we should not have succeeded in eluding the sharp eyes of our foes, had they wished to pursue us.

Soon after it grew dark, the sounds of horses' feet were heard. The braves flew to arms. We stood ready with our rifles. Before we could see any one, Uncle Jeff's voice was heard, and he and Manley rode into camp. They had found that the report of the scouts was correct, and that we could not hope to be able to get through in that direction. Accordingly, the next morning we again started, and pushed on until we reached a spot strongly guarded by rocks and trees, with a stream flowing on one side. Here Winnemak, believing himself secure from his foes, resolved to remain.

We now made preparations to separate from our Indian friends. None of them were willing to encounter the fatigue and dangers necessary to be undergone in crossing the mountains; they also evidently believed the region to be enchanted, and, if inhabited at all, to be the abode of spirits, or beings differing greatly from the human race. When Maysotta heard we were going, she begged Clarice and Rachel to remain with her; but Clarice had made up her mind to accompany us, and was fully prepared for all the difficulties we might have to encounter. Fortunately, Lieutenant Broadstreet had sufficient supplies of provisions for all our wants. We were thus not altogether destitute of the necessaries of life, for we had, I remember, even tea and coffee, sugar and salt. The lieutenant had also a very small bell-tent, the canvas of which formed scarcely half a load for a man. He himself seldom used it, but he insisted that it should be brought, to afford shelter to Clarice. Three or four Indians, moreover, agreed to accompany us as far as our baggage-mules could go, that they might convey our provisions and stores; after which we should have to carry them ourselves in knapsacks on our backs.

On parting with Winnemak, he told us that we should come back sooner than we expected, as he was sure we should never get over the mountains.

"'Where there's a will there's a way.' There is nothing like having the will to do a thing, to help one to succeed," answered Uncle Jeff.

Our guides were under the belief that the only practicable way in which they could get to the region they had heard of, was by following up a torrent which, they said, came down from the far-off snowy summits of the mountains in a succession of cataracts. For some distance we travelled through a dense pine forest, following the course of a stream into which we concluded the torrent fell. We frequently had to turn aside to avoid the numberless fallen trunks, or to dismount and lead our animals over them. We thus made but slow progress, and were compelled to encamp in the midst of the forest at a much earlier hour than would have been necessary in the open country. We kept up a blazing fire, however, and happily escaped a visit from bears, or any of the savage animals whose voices we heard round us on every side.

The next morning we moved forward, and looked out eagerly for a torrent. At length we heard the roar of tumbling waters, and making our way through the forest we came in sight of a cataract which altogether surpassed that of our own location. It appeared to be formed of several streams, which, rushing forth from the snowy heights, joined the main body, and then came leaping downwards in one vast mass of water, with a strength sufficient, it would seem, to force its way through the hardest rock. There could be no doubt that this was the very cataract we were in search of.

To carry our animals farther, would be impossible; indeed, had they been able to make their way, they would not have found sufficient grass for their sustenance in the rocky region we were approaching. We accordingly encamped on a level spot not far from the cataract. When I surveyed the wild and difficult region which we had to pass, I regretted that Clarice had accompanied us, and wished that she had remained with the Indians. Besides the fatigue which we must undergo, I feared that we might run short of provisions, and that my sister might be exposed to other hardships, which she was little able to endure.

She laughed at my fears.

"You do not know how strong I am; I shall be able to go through as much as any of you," she said. "Although I like Maysotta, I should not have been happy among her savage tribe."

The next morning we sent the animals back, and loaded ourselves with packs of provisions. Rachel carried as much as any one of us, and Clarice insisted on having a load likewise—although Manley, who made it up, took good care that it should be a very light one.

The first day's journey was not so fatiguing as we expected to find it, for we managed to wend our way upward on the slopes of the hills, avoiding the more broken and steep places. We were soon satisfied, too, that there was no risk of running short of food, for several times we came upon herds of deer; although, as we approached them without care, they scampered off before we were near enough to get a shot.

We had made our way through another pine forest, and had just turned an angle in the mountains, when suddenly before us we saw several wapiti, commonly known as the "Canada stag," one of the largest of the deer tribe. This animal is fully as large as the biggest ox I ever saw; his horns, branching in serpentine curves, being upwards of six feet from tip to tip. In colour he is reddish-brown; on the upper part of the neck the hairs are mixed with red and black, while from the shoulders and along the sides the hide is a kind of grey.

The stags stopped and gazed at us stupidly, without taking to flight, then began to utter cries which sounded wonderfully like the braying of an ass; upon which Uncle Jeff lifted his unerring rifle and brought one of them down, when the rest, taking fright, scampered off.

He and the two soldiers immediately began cutting up the animal.

"I wish we could take the hide with us, for it makes the best leather anywhere to be found," Uncle Jeff observed; "but we must not add to our loads."

As the day was now drawing to a close, we had not far to carry the meat we had just obtained; and coming to a spot near one of the numerous streams which fed the "big cataract," we encamped. As before, the small bell-tent, which Pat Sperry had carried, was erected for Clarice and Rachel; while we made our beds of fir-tops, round our camp-fire, with such shelter as our blankets and a few boughs afforded. We were too well accustomed to this sort of life, however, to consider it any hardship.

We had no longer any fear of being attacked by Indians, but it was still necessary to keep a watch by night, for it was very possible that a grizzly might take it into his head to pay us a visit, or a pack of wolves find us out; or a prowling panther might pounce down upon us, should the fire go out, and no one be on the alert to drive him off.

CHAPTER NINE

WE CONTINUE OUR JOURNEY OVER THE MOUNTAINS, AND ENCAMP IN A FERTILE VALLEY—HUNT ELK IN COMPANY WITH A PANTHER—I SPOIL THE SPORT OF THE LATTER—UNCLE JEFF WOUNDS AN ELK, WHICH IS LOST DOWN A PRECIPICE—MORE FORTUNATE AFTERWARDS—UNCLE JEFF RESOLVES TO REMAIN WITH CLARICE, RACHEL, AND PAT, WHILE MANLEY, THE SERGEANT, AND I PUSH ON—DIFFICULTIES IN CROSSING THE MOUNTAINS—MANLEY IN FEARFUL DANGER—HE ESCAPES—DESCEND TOWARDS A BROAD VALLEY—ITS WONDERFUL APPEARANCE—WE ENCAMP—THE SERGEANT NEARLY SCALDS HIS FINGERS IN A TEMPTING SPRING—CURIOUS PHENOMENON—DREADFUL NOISES OF WILD BEASTS DISTURB OUR SLUMBERS.

The next day, at an early hour, we were again on the move, Clarice and Rachel trudging on bravely with the help of long thin poles, the points hardened in the fire. Onwards and upwards we went, sometimes passing through dense forests, and climbing over the trunks of fallen trees; at others making our way through glades, where, sheltered from the sun, the walking was comparatively easy. On emerging into the more open ground, we searched for some canon or cleft in the mountains through which we might find a passage. As for going over the summits of the mountains, that was evidently impossible. They consisted of jagged pinnacles, or precipitous rocks covered with snow; and even the most experienced mountaineers, supplied with ropes and all other appliances, could not hope to surmount them.

At length, after traversing for some distance the mountain-side, we saw before us a deep gorge, at the bottom of which rushed a torrent towards the east.

"If we can find holding ground for our feet, we may get through there," said Manley.

Uncle Jeff agreed with him, so we made towards it. For ourselves we had no fears, but we naturally felt very anxious for Clarice, who must suffer from fatigue with such rough and dangerous climbing as lay before us; although, in reality, with her correct eye and active feet, she was as secure on the giddy heights and snowy ledges over which we passed as any one of us.

Poor Rachel felt the cold greatly, and was less able to get along than her young mistress. Still she persevered. "If you go I go, Missee Clarice; never mind where," said the faithful creature; although very often she crept along on her hands and knees rather than trust herself to an upright position.

Thus, climbing along the side of the precipice, with a gorge so deep on one side that the bottom was invisible, and the mountain rising on the other apparently lost in the skies, we worked our way on until, after descending again for some distance, we reached more level ground. It was a large valley or plateau surrounded by mountains; those we had crossed being on the one side, while a still more elevated range occupied the other. Wild as was the scenery through which we had passed, this was wilder still. It was traversed, however, by the stream whose course we had followed, and although we were unable to see its source, there could be no doubt that it descended from the lofty range before us. A portion of the plateau was covered by a forest, nourished by numerous rivulets, most of which flowed into larger streams, although some found an outlet towards the southward. No signs of inhabitants were visible; but game of every kind was most abundant, herds of deer, mountain sheep, and birds of all descriptions.

"I am not the man to propose going back," said Uncle Jeff; "but unless we can find an opening in these rocks, it is very clear that our present party cannot go forward. I propose, therefore, that we should camp here until we have explored the country ahead, after which we shall be able to form our plans."

He looked towards Clarice as he spoke. He had resolved not to expose her to the fatigue and peril which his experience told him must inevitably be endured by those attempting to make their way through so wild a region as that before us. He therefore selected a suitable spot for camping. Clarice's tent was put up, and we cut down poles and boughs with which to form a couple of small huts for ourselves. Uncle Jeff, Manley, and I had one, and the two men the other.

While the sergeant and Pat were employed in erecting the huts, the rest of us took our rifles and started in search of game, and before long we caught sight, towards the northern end of the valley, of several elk or moose feeding near a wood. It was necessary to approach them cautiously, however, for should they take the alarm they would be off at a rate which would give us little chance of overtaking them. But the wind came from them to us, and this was to our advantage.

The elk is one of the most wary of the deer tribe, and, notwithstanding his enormous horns, he can pass through a thick forest, as he throws them back on his shoulders so as in no way to impede his progress. Large as was the wapiti which we had before met with, the elk is still larger, and one of the animals we saw before us was fully seven feet in height—as tall, indeed, as many an elephant. As the flesh is very palatable food, we were eager to kill one or more of the herd. Uncle Jeff, too, said that he wanted the skins to assist in making a tent, in case we should have to remain some time at our present location.

Creeping along, then, as much under cover as possible, we endeavoured to get within shot of the animals. We succeeded at last in reaching the wood, and hoped, by making our way through it concealed by the trees, to get up to them before we were discovered. Uncle Jeff led the way, while Manley and I followed in Indian file. It was important not only to keep ourselves concealed, but to avoid making any noise, as the elk has a remarkably acute sense of hearing, and the slightest sound might startle the herd.

We had succeeded in gaining a spot a thousand yards or so from them, when I heard a noise in the bushes on our left, and rather ahead, the herd being on the right. On looking narrowly in the direction from whence the sound came, I caught sight of a panther, or "American lion," as the beast is commonly called, stealing along, very probably on the same errand as we were,—hoping to pounce upon one of the females of the herd, could he catch his prey unprepared. He is bound to be cautious, however, how he attacks a buck, for the elk can do battle with his horns and hoofs, and might disable even the savage panther.

Uncle Jeff saw the brute as soon as I did, and turning round, he made a sign to me to aim at the panther the moment he should fire at the elk. In the meantime, the panther was so intent on reaching his expected prey that he was not likely to observe us. As may be supposed, I kept a watchful eye on the wild beast, for he might possibly become aware of our presence; and if so, might content himself with a human being for his supper instead of venison, and I had no fancy to give him an opportunity of selection.

It was very exciting having both the panther and deer before us. Frequently Uncle Jeff stopped, fearful of being discovered by the elk; while the panther, for the same reason, did likewise. Thus the savage beast would creep on and on, crouching down and concealing himself from view. He so far interfered with our sport, that we could have the chance of killing only two deer instead of three; for I was to reserve my fire for his benefit, and I ardently hoped I should not miss. I tried to make Manley understand that it would be prudent in him not to fire until he saw whether my bullet took effect, but I could not be certain what he would do.

Our progress was now slower than ever. Several times the deer had looked up, apparently suspecting that danger was near; but still Uncle Jeff advanced, in a stooping posture, unwilling to stir even the smallest twig for fear of alarming the wary herd. I moved on more rapidly; the panther was now not more than twenty yards from us, and would in a few seconds make his deadly spring.

Suddenly Uncle Jeff stopped, raised his rifle to his shoulder, and fired. The panther at that moment was rising, about to dash forward from the brushwood. I pulled the trigger; at the same instant Manley fired—he had aimed at the deer—and as the smoke cleared away I saw the panther fall back on the ground.

The deer were now in full flight, so I followed Uncle Jeff and Manley in the direction the herd were taking towards the north end of the valley. What means they had of escape we could not tell; we hoped that, shut in by the mountain, we might again get near enough to have another shot.

The wounded elk was evidently severely hurt, for his pace now began to slacken, so Uncle Jeff cheered us on. We saw, however, that unless we could soon come up with the chase he might escape us altogether. The appearance of the country had changed, too; while rocks arose at some distance, there was evidently a vast intervening chasm between us and them.

Once more Uncle Jeff fired, but, although the bullet took effect, the deer continued his course. Almost immediately afterwards, what was our disappointment to see the wounded animal, regardless of the fate he was about to suffer, spring over the edge of a precipice, while the rest of the herd scampered away towards some almost inaccessible rocks on the left!

The elk was irretrievably lost. In vain we searched for a way by which we might reach the bottom of the gorge; we were soon convinced that the cliff was utterly impracticable.

"It can't be helped," cried Uncle Jeff; "but we must not give up the hope of obtaining some venison this evening. The elk will not long remain out on these barren rocks, and if we can hide ourselves near where they have to pass, we may each of us kill one."

We were not long in finding some thick bushes behind which we could kneel and take good aim at the passing deer.

"Do not let us be greedy," said Uncle Jeff; "you and Manley, Ralph, select one animal, and I will take another."

In half an hour or less the deer came trotting back towards their former feeding-ground, and we all three fired; Uncle Jeff knocked over a buck, and we killed a doe.

It took us some time to cut them up, and it was nearly dark before we reached the spot where I had shot the panther. Anxious to know whether it was still alive, I made my way through the wood to the place, but could nowhere find the animal. Had it escaped, notwithstanding its wound? It was too dark, however, to search for it; so we hurried on as fast as we could with our load of venison to the camp, where Clarice was eagerly looking out for us. The huts were erected by this time, and a blazing fire lighted; and I noticed that Clarice's tent had been carefully staked round by the sergeant, so that no wild beast could break suddenly into it.

"I am afraid, Miss Middlemore, that you will grow very weary of the rough life we are compelled to lead," observed Manley.

"Oh no! I enjoy it very much indeed," she answered, looking up in his face, "and shall be really sorry when it comes to an end."

"I doubt that very much, young lady," said Uncle Jeff. "We have only just commenced the passage of the mountains, and I have made up my mind not to let you go on unless some tolerably easy path can be found over them. I am very much afraid, however, that we shall not discover one fit for you to travel on."

"Then what are we to do, Uncle Jeff?" asked Clarice.

"I will tell you," he answered. "I propose remaining here with one of the men, while Lieutenant Broadstreet, the other man, and Ralph, try to make their way across the mountains.

They may manage to do it; but if they had you with them, they would probably fail—no disrespect to your prowess, so don't pout your lips."

"What do you say to my plan, lieutenant?"

"Although I would rather have Miss Middlemore's company, yet I confess that I should be often very anxious about her and her servant venturing into places through which I should not hesitate to penetrate alone. I consider your plan, therefore, under the circumstances, the best that could be adopted; and as you promise me the assistance of Ralph, I will leave Pat Sperry to attend on you—and Pat is a trustworthy fellow, when the liquor bottle is kept out of his way."

I do not think Clarice liked this plan, but she had no valid objection to urge against it; indeed, when she looked up at the snowy mountains before us, and the vast chasms which yawned on each side, she must have owned to herself that she was unfitted to travel through such a region.

Next morning we sent the two men for the deer skins, and a further supply of venison; but when they came back they brought the skin of the panther as well. They had found the animal close to the body of the deer, by the scent of which he must have been attracted; but he must have died of his wounds before he had begun to eat the flesh.

We spent the rest of the day in making pemmican, and in doing up our packages in a more compact form. The larger part of our stores we left for the party in camp—only taking powder and shot, a small quantity of coffee, and a few simple cooking utensils, so that we might travel as lightly as possible. We had little doubt about being able to obtain a sufficient supply of game; and Sergeant Custis, who was a bit of a botanist, said that he hoped to find roots which would serve as vegetables.

Early in the morning, having said good-bye to our friends, we set out. The valley was soon crossed, and we then proceeded along the base of the mountains to the southward, in the hope of finding some opening in the cliffs, or a practicable path up which we might climb. Our rifles were slung at our backs, and we each carried a long pole, on the strength of which we could thoroughly depend.

At length we came to an opening. It did not look very promising, but it was the only one which offered us any means of penetrating into the mountains, and ultimately, as we hoped, of getting over them. For some distance we kept along a ledge which gradually ascended, with a steep precipice on one side and an almost perpendicular cliff on the other. Gradually, however, the ledge became broader, and we forced our way among the trees which grew on it.

Manley proved himself an excellent mountaineer; and as I had for many years been accustomed to climbing, I ventured along paths which many would have hesitated to follow.

I cannot describe the whole of that day's journey—the dreadful precipices along which we scrambled, the profound gorges into which it almost made the head giddy to look down, the rugged heights we climbed, the thick forests of pine through which we penetrated. Still, we did not complain, hoping that success would crown our efforts.

At length we reached a place near trees and water, which would supply us with the only necessaries we required; so we built a rough shelter with boughs, for the wind was piercingly cold. We were able to defy it, however, with the help of a large fire, which we kept blazing in front of our hut.

We were making better progress than I had expected, but still range upon range of snowy mountains lay between us and the western slopes which it was our object to descend. Perhaps our trials and fatigues had only just commenced. However, none of us were inclined to give in; and as we got some sound sleep by turns, we were prepared after breakfast to set out again.

Up, up we went, the cold increasing rapidly. Every hollow below us was filled with snow; still, we could find no canon or gorge of any description through which to make our way. Over the range we must go—or, at all events, some lofty shoulder of it. We had now to encounter a new description of danger, too. The snow lay on the only practicable path, and it might conceal deep crevasses; or an avalanche might descend from above, and overwhelm us; or the mass, slipping from beneath our feet, might carry us down into one of the fathomless chasms below. Notwithstanding this, we went on and on, until it would have been as dangerous to turn back as to go forward.

I was taking the lead, when, on turning an angle of a rock, I saw spread out before me a valley so broad that my eye could scarcely reach the opposite side. Flowing through it were numerous streams; a large lake, many miles in extent, occupied its centre; while hills and forests dotted it in all directions. But, as I looked below, I saw a precipice of fearful depth, which it would be impossible to descend.

I had observed, as I came by, a steep slope leading upwards on our right, thickly covered with snow. I thought, however, that it might afford us a way by which, having ascended it, we could reach a part of the mountain from whence to descend with less risk than from that on which we now stood, so I shouted to my companions to take it. Sergeant Custis heard me, and we mounted together, expecting that

Manley would follow.

I looked round to speak to him, when what was my horror to see him gliding rapidly down, surrounded by a vast mass of crumbling snow, towards the edge of the precipice which I have just mentioned! My heart sank within me. To render him any assistance was impossible; in a few minutes he would be dashed to pieces. I should have been horrified to see any human being in so fearful a predicament; but he was my friend, the first I had ever possessed. I thought, also, of the grief the news of his death would cause my sweet sister Clarice. How should I be able to tell her of it? These thoughts flashed across my mind.

Close to the very edge of the precipice, a mass of jagged rock stood out. Already Manley had disappeared, and the snow went thundering down. For a moment I felt inclined to let myself glide down also. Just then I heard a voice; it was Manley shouting out to us not to attempt to come to his rescue. When about to be hurled over the edge of the precipice, he had clutched the jutting rock, and held on for his life, while the snow went rushing by under his feet. He waited until it had ceased to fall, and then, clutching the sides of the rock, by a powerful effort slowly worked himself upward until at last he gained the firmer part of the snow. Still, he several times cried out to us not to attempt to join him, lest our united weight might again set the mass in motion.

"I have indeed been mercifully preserved," he said, when, having rejoined us, we congratulated him on his escape. "I pray that we may succeed in getting down into the valley, although at present I see no path open to us."

After climbing some way, we found a gap in the rocks, which, although full of snow, afforded a sufficiently firm footing to enable us to get on without much difficulty. From thence, although the descent was not without danger, we succeeded in reaching a broad ledge free from snow. Here some bushes grew, of sufficient size to afford us fuel; and sheltered in the hollow of a rock, we passed the night in tolerable comfort.

On the return of day we recommenced our search for a practicable way down the mountain; and happily finding it, we at length reached one of the lower heights of the wide valley I have mentioned. I call it a valley, but it was rather a large basin, surrounded, as far as the eye could reach, by lofty mountains.

"Now we are here, how are we ever to get out again?" I asked Manley.

"Where those rivers find an outlet, so probably shall we," he answered. "There can be no doubt that two or perhaps more canons lead into this basin,—some to the north and east, so far as I can judge, and others to the west,—and by them, without having any ascent to climb, we shall probably be able to make our way in the direction we wish to go."

Having the day before us, we proceeded westward across the basin. We soon found, however, that it was anything but level. Large hills, many of which might have been dignified by the title of mountains, rose up in various directions. One object, however, engaged our attention in the far distance: it was a beautiful sheet of water, blue as the sky overhead—like a jewel in a setting of green.

Nowhere could we see any Indian wigwams, but here and there we observed what appeared like smoke rising above the trees.

"I very much doubt if what we see is smoke," observed Manley; "it looks more like vapour; and, from the appearance of this region, I suspect that some volcanic action is going forward. However, we shall discover that as we proceed."

Although we at first fancied we had reached the valley's level, we found we had still a considerable descent to make, and that we could not hope to arrive that day on the banks of the lake. We therefore encamped on the borders of a forest overlooking a stream which evidently ran into the lake, and which would serve to guide us the next day. The stream was bordered by rocks of a curious form, but we had not time to examine them before it was dark, as we had to make our usual preparations for passing the night.

Sergeant Custis at once took the can to get some water from a spring which, not for off, issued from a rock and fell into a basin. From the regular appearance of this basin, we might have supposed it to have been artificial. The sergeant dipped in his can, but he drew it back in a great hurry, exclaiming, "Why, it's at boiling heat!"

We hurried up, and found that such was indeed the case. As the water had a peculiar taste, we agreed not to use it for cooking, lest it might have some pernicious effect; so the sergeant had a considerable distance to go before he could get down to fill his can.

It had now become quite dark, and we were seated round our camp-fire, when we heard low rumbling sounds; and great was our astonishment to see, by the light of the moon, which just then appeared from behind a cloud, a lofty jet of silvery water, rising, as it seemed to us, a hundred feet or more into the air! Although our curiosity was excited, we had no wish to venture towards the spot in the darkness, as we hoped to be able to examine it the next morning.

Scarcely had we placed our heads on the fir-tops which formed our couches, when hideous sounds burst forth from the forest. The screeching of night-birds, the barking of coyotes, the dismal howling of the llovas, the cry of the panther, and other sounds, well-nigh drove sleep from our eyelids, and showed us that this region must be thickly inhabited by the wild beasts of the forest, although no human beings might be found within it. Having plenty of powder and shot, however, we were not alarmed on that account. Still, it was necessary to keep up a blazing fire, and to watch vigilantly, lest any unwelcome visitor might intrude upon us, and still more unpleasantly disturb our night's rest.

CHAPTER TEN

ADVANCE TOWARDS A BEAUTIFUL LAKE—HOT SULPHUR SPRINGS MET WITH—BOILING MUD POTS—CURIOUS BASINS FORMED BY WATER IN THE SIDE OF THE MOUNTAIN—LOVELY FRETWORK ROUND THEIR RIMS—NEARLY SINK INTO A BOILING MUD POOL—THE LAKE REACHED—ABUNDANCE OF GAME AND FISH—BUILD A RAFT—BEGIN VOYAGE ACROSS LAKE—VIOLENT STORM—IN GREAT DANGER—DRIVEN ACROSS THE LAKE—WE CLING TO TREES WHILE THE RAFT IS DASHED TO PIECES—MAKE OUR WAY THROUGH THE FOREST—I MISS MY COMPANIONS, AND LOSE MY GUN AND KNAPSACK OVER A PRECIPICE—REACH FOOT OF MOUNTAIN—I CAMP WITHOUT SUPPER OR FIRE.

In spite of the fearful noises produced by the savage inhabitants of that region, and certain slow, ominous rumbling sounds which came up from the direction of the waterspout, when we did go to sleep we slept soundly enough. At length the sergeant, who had taken the last watch, roused up Manley and me, and we started to our feet—my first impulse being to look out for the jet of water which I supposed I had seen on the previous evening, but which was now nowhere visible.

"If we have got into an enchanted land, as the Indians suppose it is, the fairies or spirits have not thought fit, during the night, to trouble us," said Manley, laughing. "Our business now is to try and make our way across this valley—so, forward!"

After breakfast, we strapped on our packs and recommenced our march, our object being to reach the shore of the lake as soon as possible. If there were any native inhabitants in this region, they would probably be found there; and we would either get them to put us across the lake in their canoes, or else we would skirt along it until we could again take a westerly course.

We soon found that we had got into a region subject to violent volcanic action, and were compelled to turn aside to avoid a wide space full of ponds, the intervals between which were covered with a crust of brimstone. I attempted to reach one of the ponds, but had not gone far when the point of my pole went through the crust, and up bubbled a quantity of black slime. On touching it, and finding it scalding hot, I shouted to my companions, who were behind, not to venture on the treacherous ground. A horror seized me, and every instant I feared that I should break through the surface. Should that take place, what a dreadful fate would be mine! I hastened back, stepping cautiously, as if moving over ice too thin to bear my weight; and very thankful I was when I once more got on hard ground.

Still further on, as we proceeded down the valley, we saw vapour rising from numerous fissures in the hill-sides. Around these vents quantities of sulphur had been deposited. But the most curious objects were basins of all sizes, nearly circular, of which there were great numbers—formed, apparently, by the lime contained in the hot springs. Some of these springs were exhausted; others, as they gushed forth from the mountain-side, were hot enough to boil potatoes. Beautiful as was the appearance of the basins, we were too eager to push forward, to examine them minutely. One was from twelve to twenty feet in diameter, and had a beautifully scalloped border. So perfect was the shading of the scallops, that it looked like a most delicate work of art rather than the production of nature. From the centre spouted up water to the height of seven or eight feet. Farther on was another boiling spring, of far greater dimensions,—a horrible-looking caldron, the water dark and muddy, and in ceaseless agitation.

"Here is a pot suitable for the witches' caldron in Macbeth," cried out Manley.

He was rather ahead of me, and on overtaking him I found him standing by the side of a circular basin whose diameter we calculated to be fully twenty feet. The contents consisted of what greatly resembled hasty pudding, or, as Manley said, "a huge caldron of thick mash." The whole surface was bubbling up every instant, and giving off a thud like the noise produced by the escape of the gas below.

Curious as these sights were, we were still more astonished by the appearance of the side of the mountain, the base of which we passed. All up the slope was seen, as it were, one above another, a succession of large basins or reservoirs. The margins were beautifully scalloped and adorned with natural bead-work of exquisite beauty. In spite of our hurry, we could not resist the temptation of making our way up to them. One of the largest springs we calculated to be fully thirty feet in diameter; and so perfectly transparent was the water, that, as we looked down into it, we could see to the very bottom. Its sides were ornamented with coral-like forms of various shades, from pure white to bright cream-yellow, while the blue sky overhead gave an azure tint to the whole surface which no art could imitate. Over several parts of the rim the water was flowing down into other basins. I climbed up and looked over into one of the pools, which was literally hanging on to the one above it like a bird's nest to a wall; while beautiful stalactites were suspended below it, caused by the water which flowed over the sides. The temperature of the water when it came out of the side of the mountain was high, but in the course of its passage from pool to pool it became gradually cooler.

"I cannot resist the temptation of taking a bath in one of these beautiful basins," exclaimed Manley.

Selecting one, I followed his example; and the sergeant was soon sitting in a third, with his head just above the water. Nothing could be more refreshing and invigorating, and when we got out we all agreed that we felt better able to continue our journey.

We found that the clear atmosphere of this region greatly deceived us as to distances, and it was not until the following day that we arrived on the shores of the lake. It was nearly evening when, after having penetrated a thick pine forest, we at length stood on its borders. Few lake-scenes could be more beautiful than that now spread out before us. The southern shore was indented with long narrow inlets, while pine-crowned promontories stretched from the base of the hills on every side. Islands of emerald hue dotted its surface, and round the margin was a sparkling belt of yellow sand. The surface, unruffled by a breath of air, was of a bright green near the shore, shading into a dark ultramarine towards the centre. Whether there were fish, we had yet to discover; but we had no fear of starving, for the whole surface of the lake swarmed with birds—swans, gulls, pelicans, geese, herons, brants, sand-hill cranes, and many varieties of ducks. An island in view was literally white with the numbers of pelicans which had taken up their abode upon it. We had also seen many other birds during the day—eagles, hawks, ravens, ospreys, prairie-chickens, grouse, mocking-birds, and woodpeckers; while we caught sight of several kinds of deer, elk, and mountain sheep. Even buffalo had made their way into the valley. Grizzly bears and panthers, too, we had good reason to fear, abounded, and were likely to be troublesome to us.

We formed our camp on the shore of the lake, where there was fuel in abundance; and taking my gun, in the course of a quarter of an hour I shot geese and ducks enough to give us an ample supper, and breakfast next morning. Manley, who was a good angler, had, in the meantime, been fitting up a rod and line—for he had brought hooks with him; and I found, when I got back, that he and the sergeant had caught a dozen salmon-trout, between a pound and a pound and a half in weight. Their colour was of a light grey above, and a pale yellow below. The dorsal and caudal fins were dark grey, and the others mostly of a brilliant orange or bright yellow.

We calculated that the lake was fully twenty miles long, and not less than fifteen broad in its widest part; and had we not been in a hurry to proceed on our journey, we agreed that we would have willingly spent some days in this enchanting spot. However, this was not to be thought of.

We kept up a blazing fire all night, and consequently escaped a visit from either grizzly or panther. The question now was, "How were we to cross the lake?" We were none of us much accustomed to boating, although Sergeant Custis knew more about it than either Manley or I. At first we talked of building a canoe, but the sergeant suggested that, as it would take some time to construct one, it would be better to form a raft, which could be put together in a few hours.

"If the water remains as quiet as it does at present, we can soon paddle to the other side; and we can also rig a mast and yard, on which we can make a very good sail with our blankets," he observed.

At daylight we commenced to build a raft. There were logs enough of every size and length in the forest, and we selected those only which we could drag with ease to the water's edge. Lithe vines, of which there were plenty hanging to the trees, served instead of ropes, and with these we bound our logs together. As the pine-wood was heavy, we formed a platform on the top of the logs with smaller poles and lighter branches, interwoven, and bound together as tightly as we considered necessary for the easy voyage we proposed to undertake.

We were, it must be understood, at the north-east end of the lake. On the west side was the promontory which we hoped to reach, and beyond it a deep gulf ran up the shore, the farther end of which we could not distinguish.

Some hours were passed in constructing the raft. We had then to cut out the paddles, a long oar to steer by, and also the mast and yard. These, although they were very roughly formed, occupied us some time longer, so that it was late in the day before we were ready to commence our voyage. We calculated, however, that we should have no difficulty in getting across before sundown; and as the evening promised to be calm and beautiful, we expected to have a pleasant passage. The wind, too, was favourable, blowing from the eastward, and would help us along,—although, as it was very light, we must be prepared to use our paddles.

The raft had been built in the water, so that all we had to do was to step on board, set our sail, and shove off. "Away we go!" cried Manley, giving a shove with the steering oar, and we glided off from the shore.

Sergeant Custis quickly set the sail, which, as we got a little way on, blew out with the breeze. He and I then plied the paddles. We appeared to be making fair progress, too, although the raft moved but slowly. But the wind soon dying away, we had our paddles alone to depend on. Manley tried to scull with the oar, but he was not an adept at the art, and it did not help us much. When we watched the shore we had left, we saw that we had made some progress; but when we looked ahead towards the side of the lake we wished to reach, it appeared no nearer than when we stood on the shore we had left, while the mountains rose towering up above our heads as gigantic as ever. The sun had already disappeared beyond the pine-clad heights to the west, leaving the valley in rapidly increasing shade.

"I doubt, Ralph, whether we shall set foot on shore much before midnight, unless we move at a faster rate than we are now doing," said Manley.

I agreed with him; observing, however, that a moonlight voyage on that calm lake would be pleasant in the extreme, and a thing to be remembered.

Not expecting to be so long on the raft, and intending to have supper on our arrival, we grew very hungry. Fortunately we had plenty of cooked provisions, and fresh water alongside, so that we had no difficulty in satisfying our appetites.

While the sergeant was engaged in again doing up the pack, a sudden squall struck our sail, carrying away the mast, and had I not sprung up and seized hold of it, the blanket would have been lost. Fortunately I caught it before it was wet. This squall was quickly followed by another, and we could see the white-topped waves curling up around us on all sides. Our raft was but ill calculated to buffet with a tempest such as seemed but too likely to come on. The wind being as yet favourable, however, the sergeant attempted to repair the mast and re-hoist the sail; but scarcely had he done so when it was again carried away.

"We must trust to our paddles, and the wind will still drive us along," said Manley.

We could hear the wind roaring among the trees on the shore, and every instant it increased, raising up big waves which threatened to sweep over us. The raft was tossed and tumbled about, and sometimes it was with difficulty we could hold on sufficiently to prevent ourselves from being shaken off into the seething water. We had, fortunately, at the suggestion of the sergeant, secured our rifles and knapsacks to the top of the platform in the centre of the raft, where they were tolerably secure.

We were now driving on much faster than we had hitherto been doing, but the darkness prevented us from knowing whether it was in the right direction, for we could see only the foaming waters dancing up around us. All we could do, therefore, was to hold on, and try with the steering oar to keep the raft before the wind, hoping that we might be driven into some sheltered bay, where we could land in safety.

I thought of what Clarice would have said, if she had been with us—"Trust in God"—and I felt sure that she would not have been more alarmed than we were. We saw our danger,—we could not be blind to that,—but none of us gave way to cowardly fears. Manley sat with perfect calmness, steering, while Sergeant Custis and I paddled away, endeavouring to keep the raft before the following seas. At last I caught sight of some dark object rising out of the water, but instead of being ahead, it was on the right hand, or, as we

judged, to the northward of us. It was evidently land, but whether the end of the island we had seen in that part of the lake, or the mainland, we could not determine. In vain we attempted to paddle up to it; the gale drove us on, and showed us that we were perfectly unable to go in any direction excepting that towards which the wind should impel us.

Again we lost sight of the land, and this led us to think that we must have passed an island. The waves hissed and foamed, and danced up around us as much as ever; still our raft held together, and we were enabled to cling on to it. Even if we were only moving at the rate of two miles an hour, it could not take us more than seven or eight hours to get across from one side of the lake to the other, and we calculated that we must already have been that time on the raft. What if we had got into a channel of some river, which might rush rapidly along, pouring over some terrific cataract? Should we by any means be able to reach the shore, so as to escape being carried along with the raft? Had it been daylight, the danger would not have been so great, for we might have seen in what direction to direct our efforts. As it was, we might, should we paddle to one side or the other, be placing ourselves in greater danger than by allowing the raft to drive on before the gale. Our ears were assailed by the continued roar of the waves dashing on the shore, of the wind rushing through the trees, and of the foaming waters as they clashed against each other; we sometimes, indeed, could scarcely hear each other's voices. There being now no sail, we were able to keep our eyes turning in every direction.

"When we do reach the shore, we must take care not to lose our things," said Manley, with due thought. "Let each man seize his rifle and knapsack; for if we fail to get into a harbour, we shall probably be dashed against a rocky shore, or among overhanging trees, where our raft will, no doubt, quickly be knocked to pieces."

Dangerous as was our present position, we had to confess that the operation of landing might prove even more perilous; still we were eager to go through it, trusting that, notwithstanding the danger, we should escape.

At length Sergeant Custis cried out, "Land ahead! We shall be close to it in a few minutes. It seems to me to be covered with wood, with mountains rising beyond. Yes! no doubt about it! We must each try to get hold of a stout branch or trunk of a tree, and cling on to it until daylight returns and we can see our way."

The sergeant was right, although the time we took to reach the shore was longer than he expected it would be. In daylight we could have made our escape without difficulty, but now we ran the most fearful risk of being crushed against the raft, as it surged up and down; or against the trees, which hung, some with their branches in the water, others but slightly raised above it, while the seething waters whirled and leapt around their trunks with a force which must soon reduce our raft to fragments.

"Now is our time!" cried the sergeant. "Quick, quick, gentlemen!" and seizing a branch, he swung himself up into a tree, hauling his rifle and knapsack after him. The next instant he extended his hand to me, by which assistance I was enabled to follow his example. On looking round, I lost sight of Manley. Had he been washed off, or struck by a bough?

"Manley, Manley!" I shouted; "where are you?"

"All right!" he answered, greatly to my relief.

The sound came from a distance, for even after I had left the raft it had been driven some way on before he could manage to grasp a bough. We had at all events succeeded in our object of crossing the lake, although we had not landed exactly in the manner we desired, nor could we tell our whereabouts. We might be at the very southern end of the lake, should the wind have shifted to the northward, or we might be at its western extremity. Wherever we were, there we must remain until daylight; for were we to attempt moving, in the pitchy darkness which hung around, we might fall off into the water, or lose ourselves in the forest.

"It cannot be far off daylight, sergeant," I observed.

"I think not," he answered; "but I would advise you to take care not to drop off to sleep. If you do, you may chance to fall into the water. It will be as well to caution the lieutenant, or he, being alone, may forget himself."

Considering the noise of the waves dashing under our feet, the waving of the trees, and the howling of the wind amid them, I did not think the caution very necessary; but, notwithstanding, I shouted out to Manley.

"No fear of that," he answered. "It would require a more comfortable spot for a bivouac, to induce me to take a snooze."

That night appeared to me the longest I can remember. Days appeared to have passed since we had left the eastern shore, with the bright sunlight and the calm blue water. Still, day must return. What a comfort that thought often is! The roar of the waters gradually decreased, the wind having fallen, and thus, in spite of the sergeant's warning, my head was beginning to nod, when he cried out—

"Here is daylight at last; I see a tint of red over the snowy tops of the mountains. We shall have the sun himself sending his warm rays down upon us before long."

His voice aroused me in a moment Manley answered his hail; and as the light increased we saw that we were at the farther end of what might be the main body of the lake, or a branch running off it. It was in reality the great western arm of the lake, and we had been carried many miles on our journey, in the exact direction we wished to go.

We had soon light enough to enable us to crawl off the branches to which we had clung, and make our way down to the ground—if ground it could be called, for, in reality, in every direction it was covered thickly with logs in all stages of decay, some only lately fallen, others which could be knocked to pieces with a kick, while the feet sank at almost every step in decomposed vegetable matter. Still this was the region through which, somehow or other, we must make our way.

After an hour's toil we reached a small open space, where the ground was sufficiently hard to enable us to light a fire and dry our drenched clothes and blankets. We had also to look to the priming of our rifles, as they were likely to have got damp, and might fail us at a pinch. Being unwilling to encamp in the forest altogether, though we all greatly required rest, we resolved to push on until we could reach more open ground where water was to be obtained.

To save my companions labour, as I was a more practised backwoodsman than either of them, I offered to go ahead and try to find the shortest way out of the forest. How far it might be, I could not tell; but I had hopes that the forest in which we were might prove to be only a belt of trees on the shore of the lake.

It did not occur to me as possible that my companions could miss my trail. I shouted now and then, however, but did not hear their voices in reply, the forest being so dense that sounds could not penetrate far through it I went on and on, feeling sure that I was directing my course to the westward. The ground rose more and more, too, in some places rather abruptly, but still covered with a dense growth of trees, and soon I found that I was mounting a hill. The path was more easy than at first, however, there being but few fallen trunks, so I made much better progress.

"I must get out of this," at last I said to myself; and so I continued moving on, occasionally notching a tree with my axe, if I thought my trail was not sufficiently distinct. "Of course they will follow," I thought more than once. I did not, indeed, entertain a doubt about it.

I had reached the top of the hill, but the trees were too high to enable me to see any of the country around. I could judge by the direction of the sun's rays, however,—which had now drawn round, and were striking in my face,—that I was steering westward, as before. I occasionally stopped and looked back, expecting that my friends would overtake me; and although I did not see them, I felt so sure that they must be close behind that I continued my course.

On and on I went, when again I found myself descending, and thus knew that I had crossed over a hill of some height; still the trees prevented me from getting a view of the country beyond. At last I came to some marshy ground of a similar character to that which I had met on the other side of the lake, with sulphur springs in the centre. I had therefore to make a detour to avoid it, but as the tall trees which grew on the surrounding hills would not allow me to get a view of the country, I could not determine in what direction to steer my course. I did not perceive an important circumstance. Owing to the spongy nature of the ground, into which my feet sank at every step, the marks were soon obliterated, while I still supposed that my trail was sufficiently defined to enable Manley and the sergeant to follow me.

I now mounted another hill, of a far more rugged character than the former ones which I had passed over.

"Surely," I thought, "on the other side of this there must be open ground, where I shall be able to see my way ahead, and select a spot for our camp." The hill, however, proved to be even more rugged than I had expected. Still I did not like to go back, though the farther I went the wilder and more jagged it became.

At last I found myself scrambling along the summit of a precipice, until I saw before me a foaming cascade falling down the precipitous rocks, with lofty pinnacles rising above it. This formed a cataract which, after a short course, ran into a lakelet at the foot of the cliffs; while beyond was the open ground I had been hoping to find.

Although a good cragsman, my climb had been a rough one, and I now sat down to rest on the top of the cliff before I commenced mounting higher, which it was necessary to do in order to get above the falls, and from thence make my way down the further side of the mountain on to the open ground. To rest my shoulders, I had taken off my pack, and placed it with my rifle by my side. I failed to notice, as I did so, the slippery nature of the rock, which was covered with a velvet-like surface of moss, produced by the constant spray from the waterfall. Feeling thirsty, I thought that I could reach a small jet of water which, flowing amid the rocks, fell into the main cascade. I therefore got up to make my way to it, and while doing so must have touched my rifle with my foot I obtained the water, although not without difficulty, and more danger than it was wise to run for the purpose. But, on returning, what was my dismay to see neither rifle nor knapsack! They had both, it was very evident, slipped over the cliff, and fallen into the lakelet. Had I been alone, my loss would have been indeed a serious one, but as I hoped that my friends would soon overtake me, I did not allow it to depress my spirits.

I approached as near to the edge of the cliff as I dared, thinking it possible that my rifle and knapsack might have fallen on some ledge, or perhaps been stopped in their downward progress by bushes; but, as far as I could judge, the precipice was perpendicular, and they must have fallen into the lakelet. I saw at once, therefore, that there was very little chance of my being able to recover them; still that point could not be decided until I got down to the level of the lake, when I might ascertain its depth. If not very deep, I might perhaps be able to dive to the bottom; but though naturally eager to make the attempt, I felt it would be safest to do nothing in the matter until I was joined by my friends.

I waited a short time for their coming up, but as they did not appear, I thought it desirable to retrace my steps, in case they should have missed their way, or lost sight of my trail. I accordingly went back, shouting out to them; but it was not until I came to the spongy ground I had passed, that I saw the probability of their having lost my trail and gone in some other direction. In vain I searched for signs of them. Should I return to where I parted from them, a long time might elapse before we might meet; and my anxiety to try and recover my rifle and knapsack forbade me doing this.

The day was advancing, and darkness would come on before I could get to the shore of the lake, so I again turned and made my way over the mountain till I got above the fall; from thence, with infinite labour and at no little risk, I ultimately succeeded in reaching the level ground. I had now to go round the base of the mountain in order to reach the lake; but the distance was considerable, and I could scarcely hope to reach it before nightfall. I felt, therefore, that it would be prudent to look out for a spot for camping. A grove of trees of no great extent was before me, and their trunks would afford shelter; but what about a fire? My flint and steel I had incautiously left in my knapsack, but I had a small burning-glass which one of our visitors at the farm had given me. I had seldom made use of it, but I had put it in my pocket, with the few valuables I possessed, on the night we left Roaring Water. As the sun had disappeared, that, however, would be of no use for the present; so I arrived at the unsatisfactory conclusion that I must pass the night without food or fire.

CHAPTER ELEVEN

ALONE IN THE FOREST—AWAKENED BY THE CRY OF A PANTHER—THE BRUTE DISCOVERS ME—I TAKE REFUGE IN A TREE—THE PANTHER DISAPPEARS—A VISIT TO THE LAKE—VAIN EFFORTS TO RECOVER MY RIFLE AND KNAPSACK—I CONTINUE TOWARDS THE WEST, HOPING TO MEET MY FRIENDS—MORE SULPHUR SPRINGS—NEARLY OVERWHELMED BY A MUD VOLCANO—A POISONOUS VALLEY—CAUGHT IN A SNOW-STORM—BUILD A HUT—MY FARE, THISTLE ROOTS—MAKE TRAPS AND A FISHING-LINE—SALLY FORTH—CATCH THREE BEAVERS—FIND ANOTHER LAKE—SALMON-TROUT CAUGHT—CONTINUE DOWN A RIVER, AND COME UPON A NUMBER OF MAGNIFICENT GEYSERS—AM ABOUT TO TAKE UP MY ABODE IN A GROTTO, WHEN A HOT SPRING RISES FROM IT—I SHIFT MY QUARTERS—PREPARE FOR ANOTHER SOLITARY NIGHT—I HEAR A SHOT, AND A WOUNDED DEER BOUNDS NEAR ME.

My exertions had made me hungry. Recollecting the amount of animal life which abounded in that region, however, I had no great fear of starving altogether, for if I could not shoot I might trap animals. I hoped, however, to be able to rejoin my companions the following day, when my wants would be supplied, so that I was not much out of spirits. Should I fail to trap game at any time, or should I fail to meet my companions even for some days, there were, I remembered, roots of various sorts which might serve for food, though it was now too late to obtain them. Indeed, barely light enough remained to enable me to cut down some branches with which to form a slight hut. I managed to collect a few to answer my purpose, the thick trunk of a tree serving as a back. In spite of this shelter, it was very cold; but of course I made up my mind to endure it as best I could, and, in spite of hunger and anxiety, it was not long before I fell asleep.

What time had elapsed I know not, when I was awakened by a shrill cry, almost like that of a human being. I shouted out for help before I was quite awake, thinking it must come from my companions, who were in danger; but when completely aroused, I knew too well that it was the shriek of the panther which so often makes night hideous in the forests of the south. What the brute was about, I could not tell; but as I knew he must be close to me, I again shouted out, hoping to frighten him away. At the same time clutching hold of a low branch of the tree which hung directly overhead, I swung myself into it.

Presently I saw the panther come out of a thicket close at hand, and smell round the hut. He had only just discovered me, and seemed to have a strong inclination to make his supper off my body. I did not feel altogether comfortable, even where I was, as I had a belief that panthers can climb, like most of the cat tribe, and that he might take it into his head to mount the tree. I had no weapon besides my knife, but with that I managed to cut off a pretty thick branch, with which I hoped to be able to defend myself.

As I found it very cold where I sat, my first object was to try and drive the brute away. I therefore kept pelting him with pieces of withered branches, which I broke off; but to no purpose. Still snarling occasionally, he kept smelling round and round the tree, frequently casting a look up at me with his glittering eyes. Now and then he went to a little distance, and seemed about to spring into the tree. At last he got into a position which enabled me to take good aim at him, and I threw a heavy piece of a branch, which hit him directly on the nose. At the same time I sprung round the tree, so as to be concealed from his view. He gave an upward glance; but not seeing me, he appeared to be seized with sudden fright, and, greatly to my satisfaction, went muttering away into the depths of the wood.

Trusting that the panther would not come back, I descended the tree, and once more sought the shelter from which he had driven me. The interruption to the night's repose had been somewhat unpleasant, but that did not prevent me sleeping on until daylight; after which I proceeded in the direction where I expected to find the lakelet into which my rifle and knapsack had dropped.

I was considering what I should do for food, when I observed a green plant of a bright hue, with a small head, which I recognised as a thistle, the roots of which I had seen the Indians use for food. Pulling it up, I found it not unlike a radish in taste and consistency. Searching about, I soon found several more: and although not likely to be very nutritious, the roots served to stop the gnawings of hunger, and enabled me to make my way with a more elastic step.

My thoughts were occupied as to the probability of finding Manley and the sergeant. I hoped that, once clear of the forest, they might encamp and make a large fire, the smoke of which would serve to guide me to them. Should they, on the contrary, continue searching about, we might miss each other.

The shore of the lakelet was at last reached, but my first glance at it convinced me that there was every probability of its being of great depth. The cliffs over which my rifle and knapsack had fallen went sheer down into it; while farther on the torrent brought a large supply of water, which found an exit on the opposite side. The water was clear as crystal, and from the shore upon which I stood I could see the bottom. When I put in my stick, however, I could not fathom it—and this at the shallowest part. Still, my existence might depend upon recovering my rifle, so, throwing off my clothes, I plunged in and swam to the foot of the cliff. I felt sure that I was under the very spot from whence the things had fallen, but when I looked down, notwithstanding the clearness of the water, I could not see them, nor the bottom, and this at once convinced me of the immense depth. I had therefore to abandon all hope of recovering my rifle and knapsack, and swim back, not altogether without some fear of being seized with cramp from the coldness of the water.

Quickly dressing, I ran on to warm myself, keeping as before to the west, as I felt sure that Manley and the sergeant would proceed in the same direction. Coming to a high mound or hill, I climbed to the top, whence I could obtain a pretty extensive view; but nowhere could I see any objects moving which could be my friends. A herd of elk were browsing in the far distance, and a number of mountain sheep were scampering about on the side of the neighbouring height. My eyes were attracted, however, by some wreaths of vapour far down the valley, in the direction which it was probable Manley and the sergeant had taken. The vapour might arise from a fire they had kindled; but when I looked again, I saw not only one, but several wreaths, or rather jets, which made me fear that my first conjecture was wrong. However, as these jets appeared in the right direction, I determined to go towards them.

I descended from the height, and continued my course, feeling unusually weak and weary, when, some way along the valley, I observed several circular holes, full of mud of different colours bubbling up, while vapour issued from various fissures in the sides of the hills, and a sulphureous odour pervaded the air.

Becoming more and more fatigued, at last I threw myself on the ground, and ate a few of the thistle roots which I had fortunately brought with me. I remember noticing a large hole not far off, but it appeared to be empty. I felt very drowsy, and dropped off to sleep before long, my head resting on my knees; when suddenly I became conscious of a loud rumbling sound, while the earth beneath me seemed to shake and upheave.

Springing to my feet, what was my horror to see, close to me, a mass of dark water and mud rising up in the shape of a column! Higher and higher it rose, surrounded by volumes of vapour; while from its summit was scattered far and wide thick lumps of mud. Becoming aware that I had been sleeping close to an active mud geyser, I sprang away from the dangerous neighbourhood, narrowly escaping being overwhelmed with the hot and horrible mixture. The spout, or column, I should think, must have risen to a height of nearly fifty feet; while every few seconds loud reports were heard, and with each report a dense volume of steam shot forth—the ground meanwhile shaking violently.

I stood watching it till, gradually decreasing, the centre part of the column sank down into the orifice from which it had been expelled; and within a short time all was again quiet. The mass of mud which covered the ground, and coated even the boughs of the neighbouring trees, alone showed the violent outbreak that had just taken place.

As I advanced the valley began to narrow. Miasmatic vapours, escaping from holes and crevices on either side, filled the air, making it difficult to breathe with freedom, so I hastened on, anxious to get out of so horrible a region. To escape from it I climbed a hill, along the side of which I made my way as fast as the uneven nature of the ground and fallen logs and rocks would allow.

I again got into a more open country, where I became conscious of a considerable change in the atmosphere. Hitherto the air had been tolerably warm, though bracing; it now grew sensibly cooler. Thick clouds were gathering in the sky. The wind, before a gentle breeze, now rose rapidly, and blew with violence. It soon became icy cold, and flakes of snow began to fall. Without a fire, I felt I should well-nigh perish. At all events, before I could make a fire I must search for some cavern in which to light it; or, failing to find a cavern, I must build a hut. As the appearance of the ground did not indicate that caverns were likely to exist on the side of the hill, I set to work without delay to collect materials for building a hut; and having cut down a number of pine branches, I stuck them in the ground, weaving their tops together with vines, and piling as many rough pieces of bark against the side as I could find.

In vain I watched for a gleam of sunshine, which would enable me, by means of my burning-glass, to kindle a fire. The clouds gathered thicker and thicker; and no hope remained of my being able to obtain the desired spark. Taking advantage, therefore, of the remaining light, I searched about and pulled up all the thistle roots I could find. With this hermit-like fare, the only provender I was likely to obtain while the storm lasted, I retired into my hut.

Scarcely had I got under shelter when down came the snow, and the whole face of the country was speedily covered with a sheet of white. How long the storm might last, I could not tell; it might blow over in one or two hours, or days might elapse before it ceased. It was too early in the year, however, to fear the setting in of winter weather, even in that elevated region, or my condition would indeed have been deplorable.

I had kept an opening through which I could look over the valley, in case my friends might pass that way. But night came on, and they did not appear; so, closing up my window, I coiled myself away to sleep, as the size of my hut would not allow me to stretch myself at full length.

I had little fear that a panther would break into my bower; but I was not so confident that, should a grizzly scent me out, he might not poke in his nose. Still I could trust to Him who had hitherto protected me. I had my knife and my long stick, and, at all events, I might give Master Bruin an unpleasant scratch on the snout, should he come within my reach.

Notwithstanding my uncomfortable position, I was soon asleep, and did not awake until daybreak. Had I possessed any means of cooking my roots, I might have made a tolerably satisfactory breakfast. Indeed, although they assisted to sustain life, they were far from wholesome raw; still, to quell the cravings of hunger, I ate them.

The storm continued to blow with as much violence as on the previous evening, and, lightly clad as I was, I felt that it would be rash to continue my course till it was over. I sincerely hoped that Manley and the sergeant had found suitable shelter. However, as they could light a fire, and had abundance of food, I was pleased to think that they were better off than I was.

To employ the time, I tried to manufacture some traps of such materials as I possessed. I then bethought me that I had a fish-hook in my pocket; but when I came to search for a line I could find none. I had, however, a silk neckerchief; and having unravelled this, I twisted it with the greatest care into a strong thread. It occupied a good deal of time, but I succeeded in three or four hours in forming a line of sufficient length for my purpose. I had plenty of loose shot, too, which I split for weights. I then carefully rolled up the line round a piece of wood, ready for use as soon as I should reach a lake or stream likely to contain trout.

The storm lasted upwards of two days. Although my journey was thus delayed, I felt sure my friends would likewise have been prevented from travelling, and thus I was none the less likely to meet them. At length the wind subsided, the clouds dispersed, and the sun shone forth with dazzling brightness on the snow, which began quickly to disappear beneath his rays.

Carrying the traps I had manufactured, and my fishing-line, I now sallied out. I had exhausted all my roots, but as the snow cleared away I obtained a further supply, though, hungry as I was, I still had very little inclination to eat them raw.

I had not gone far when I came to some boiling springs; one of which, although the water was of intense heat, was little larger than a good-sized caldron. I threw in my roots, and sat down beside it to warm my feet, which were benumbed with the melting snow. While my frugal dinner was cooking, I looked about in search of my friends; but again I was disappointed. When I thought that the roots were sufficiently boiled, I raked them out with my stick. They were certainly more palatable, and I hoped they would prove more nutritious.

Every hour was now of importance, for Manley and the sergeant would, I calculated, be pushing on, under the belief that I was before them. I had quenched my thirst with snow, for in that volcanic region I could find no water fit to drink; it was either intensely hot, or so impregnated with sulphur and other minerals that I was afraid to swallow it. I saw that it would soon be necessary again to camp, so, that I might not have to pass the night without a fire, I endeavoured to obtain a light by means of my burning-glass, before the sun should descend too low. The wood around was so wet that I feared, after all, I should not succeed; but having made my way to a forest on one side of the valley, I discovered some moss growing under the branches of a tree which had sheltered it from the wet. Here also was abundance of dead wood. With as much as I could carry I hurried back into the open, and sitting down, brought the glass to bear on the now fast sinking rays of the sun. I watched the effect with almost trembling eagerness, till, greatly to my joy, from the small bright spot caused by the concentrated rays a thin thread of smoke began to ascend and spread over the moss. This I blew gently, placing over it a few twigs at a time, until I soon had a brisk fire burning.

The place where I had lighted my fire was not one at which I wished to camp, but once having a fire, I could carry a burning brand and ignite another in some more convenient situation. I was not long in selecting a spot close under a rock, where I soon had a fire blazing up. I thus had warmth, although I was still destitute of wholesome food; and, indeed, I found myself weaker than I had ever before been.

I was not of a disposition to give way to despondency, but sombre thoughts would intrude. I began to fear that I might not be able to rejoin my friends; that they, unable to find me, would suppose that I had met with some accident, and would at length make their way to the fort by themselves. Had I possessed my rifle and knapsack, I should have had no fear on the subject, but the only means I had of obtaining food were precarious; and I could not cast off the thought that, should I continue to grow weaker, I might ultimately perish.

I was soon shown, however, that I ought not to have desponded. I was more successful with my beaver traps than I had expected; and, imperfectly formed as they were, I caught no less than three animals in them, which afforded me ample food, and greatly restored my strength.

Pushing on over a wooded height, I saw below me a beautiful lake two or three miles long, and almost as many broad. I hastened down to its shore, and having caught some grasshoppers on the way, I quickly had my line in the water. Having chosen a favourable spot, scarcely a moment had passed before I hauled out a salmon-trout a pound or more in weight. In half an hour I had caught a dozen—as many as I could carry. I therefore camped and cooked some of the fish, which afforded me a more satisfactory supper than I had eaten for many days.

Seeing a stream running out of the lake, I next morning followed its course. I cannot describe the beautiful waterfalls which I passed on my way, or the scenery, which was altogether very fine. I hastened along, believing that the stream, from the direction it took, would lead to an outlet among the mountains.

I had thus gone on for some miles, when the canon down which I was travelling widened, and suddenly I saw before me a scene far more wonderful than any I had yet witnessed. In every direction over the broad valley, on both sides of the stream, rose a number of jets of sparkling water far surpassing in beauty the artificial fountains in the most celebrated gardens of royal mansions.

I hurried on, to get a more perfect sight of this wonderful region. Suddenly, from a high mound some thirty feet or more above the level of the plain, I saw a jet burst forth, which rose to the height of one hundred and twenty or one hundred and thirty feet—a perfect geyser, the first real one I had yet seen. It continued playing for fifteen minutes or more, the mass of water falling back into the basin, and then running over the edges and down the sides of the mound. Others were playing all the time. As I hastened on, from another cone a column shot upwards to a far greater height—considerably above two hundred feet, I should say—and lasted very much longer than the first. The intervening spaces between these geysers were covered with grass; and in many places trees rich with foliage grew luxuriantly, showing that there was no danger in venturing among them.

Another beautiful geyser, which burst up when I was not more than a hundred yards from it, had the exact appearance of a fan. On examining it, I found that it possessed a double orifice, which discharged five radiating jets to the height of sixty feet; the drops of spray as they fell perfectly representing the feathers of a fan. Nothing could be more beautiful than the effect. The eruption lasted nearly thirty minutes, the water preserving its elegant form during the whole time. About forty feet from it dense masses of vapour ascended from a hole, emitting at the same time loud sharp reports. As I looked along the river I saw small craters of every conceivable form; some were quiescent, while others poured out cascades forming small rivulets which ran into the river.

So beautiful and curious was the scene, that for a time I forgot my perilous position.

I had no fear of starving, as long as I had my fishing-line and traps, and was able to light a fire; but I knew that I had a wild and rugged road to pursue, and probably snow-capped mountains to climb, before I could reach the western plains. It was important, therefore, to obtain substantial fare, that I might regain my full strength for the undertaking. I had not, of course, given up all hope of falling in with my friends, but still I was forced to contemplate the possibility of missing them. I wondered that we had not yet met, as I certainly thought they would have taken the same direction that I had followed.

I must, at all events, spend another night in the valley; and I was looking about for some place which would afford me shelter, when I saw, a short distance off, what appeared to be a beautiful grotto—consisting of fantastic arches, pillars, and turrets, with hollows beneath them, in one of which I might find a comfortable sleeping-place. I determined to explore it, and, after collecting wood for a fire, to take my rod and line and endeavour to catch some fish in the river. I should, at all events, have no difficulty in cooking them in one of the numerous boiling caldrons in the neighbourhood. Directly behind the grotto was a forest of firs, from which I could collect an ample supply of wood for my fire, as also small branches to form my couch, should the ground prove damp.

I was making my way towards the grotto, when I heard a rumbling sound, and directly afterwards two jets of water spouted from its midst—one of them rising rapidly to the height of nearly a hundred feet, when, spreading out, down it came, the scalding water falling in a dense shower on every side, while wreaths of steam were ejected from the various holes which had been within their influence, the which would speedily have parboiled me, had I not at once run off to a safe distance. I then turned back to look at the beautiful phenomenon. Although the jet was not so lofty as many of the other geysers, its form was not less beautiful, assuming, as it curled over, the appearance of a gigantic ostrich feather.

I had received a lesson not to trust to appearances, and was now very unwilling to take up my lodgings in any one of the curious grottoes which lay scattered about in the valley. They might be perfectly quiet, and afford me comfortable shelter; or, proving treacherous, a stream of hot water might burst forth from some unperceived vent and blow me fifty feet into the air, or scald me to death. I accordingly resolved to build myself a bower in which, although it would not afford me so much shelter as a cavern, I might pass the night in safety.

It was necessary, however, before the sun should disappear, to light my fire; and having fixed upon a spot, I repaired to the woods nearest at hand to collect the fuel I had not gone far when I saw rising before me a curious white mound, twenty-five or thirty feet in height, and about a hundred at the base. From the summit rose a small puff of steam, like that escaping from the lid of a kettle; but I saw, from the appearance of the trees around it, that it could not for many years have sent forth any dangerous stream of hot water. Not far off was a small basin with an elegantly scalloped rim; it was full of hot water, which scarcely bubbled over. "This will make me a capital fish-kettle," I said to myself, "so I will build my hut near here. I do not think there can be any risk."

Having selected a clear spot, I set to work and piled up the wood for my fire. This was the first operation. I could build my hut in the dusk, or even by the light of the fire, should it be necessary, after I had caught my fish. Then taking a handful of moss into the open, with a few dry sticks, I quickly lighted it with my burning-glass, and carrying it back, soon had my fire in a blaze. I next made it up carefully, that it might burn until I came back, and hurried down to the river. I was doubtful whether trout were to be found in water into which hot streams were constantly pouring; however, as most of them became cold before they reached the main current, I thought it possible that I might be successful. In the expectation of catching fish, I had omitted to set my traps; or rather, occupied by the wonderful scenes around me, I had forgotten all about the matter. In vain I threw in my line, baited with an active grasshopper; not a fish would bite. I went higher up the river, where fewer hot springs ran into it, but I was equally unsuccessful.

The shadows beginning to spread over the valley warned me that I must return to my camping-ground and content myself with a few thistle roots for supper; and I had just wound up my line, when my ear caught the sound of what appeared to be a shot fired at some distance up the valley. It was so faint, however, that I thought it might possibly be a sound emitted by some geyser or fire-hole. Just then a deer came bounding along, a short distance off. On seeing me it swerved slightly out of its course, and as it did so I perceived a stream of blood flowing from its side.

"That *was* a shot, then!" I exclaimed; "and my friends must have fired it."

My first impulse was to run in the direction from whence the shot came, but on looking at the deer I perceived that it was slackening its pace; and after a few more bounds, down it sank to the ground, not one hundred yards from me.

CHAPTER TWELVE

I KILL THE DEER—MORE WONDERS—MEET MANLEY AND SERGEANT CUSTIS AT LAST—A PLEASANT EVENING—PARCHED WITH THIRST AMIDST SPARKLING STREAMS—OUR HAZARDOUS JOURNEY OVER THE MOUNTAINS—SAFE ARRIVAL AT FORT HARWOOD—WELCOMED BY THE COMMANDANT—AN EXPEDITION ORGANISED TO DRIVE THE INDIANS FROM THE COUNTRY—MANLEY COMMANDS IT—I ACCOMPANY HIM—MEET BARNEY AND KLITZ, STILL BOUND FOR CALIFORNIA—BARNEY GIVES AN ACCOUNT OF THEIR ESCAPE—THEIR JOURNEY STOPPED—THEY RETURN WITH US—WE MEET PIOMINGO AND HIS SQUAW—TELLS US THAT HE HAS BURIED THE WAR-HATCHET—HEAR AN ALARMING ACCOUNT OF BARTLE—ASCEND THE MOUNTAIN TO WHERE WE LEFT UNCLE JEFF—FIND HIM AND CLARICE WELL—HE HAS OBTAINED A LARGE SUPPLY OF PELTRIES—OUR RETURN TO WINNEMAK'S CAMP—MAYSOTTA ACCOMPANIES CLARICE TO ROARING WATER.

Although I had not forgotten the friends I hoped soon to see, my instinct as a hunter made me anxious to secure the deer, as it might possibly get up again, and be lost to us by springing into the river. Acting on this impulse, therefore, I ran up to the wounded animal. The poor brute was endeavouring to rise on its knees, so, ham-stringing it with my knife, I effectually prevented it from escaping. I had, however, to approach it cautiously, for a blow from its antlers, even in its present state, might prove dangerous. I managed at length to reach its throat, when its struggles speedily ceased.

I now looked round for my friends, in the expectation of seeing them at any moment, for I was sure they would follow the deer; but they did not come. Still I could not have been mistaken. The animal had been shot by a rifle bullet; it was a rifle I had heard fired. Had Indian hunters shot the deer, they would certainly have followed more closely at its heels; and besides, they were not likely to have rifles.

After having secured the deer, I hastened in the direction from whence it had come, expecting that every moment would solve the mystery. Yet, eager as I was, my eyes could not avoid remarking the wonderful objects around me. On one side was a basin, its projecting rim carved with marvellously intricate tracery, while the waters within were tinted with all the colours of the rainbow. On the other side appeared a mass greatly resembling an ancient castle. It rose more than forty feet above the plain, while in its midst was a turret of still greater dimensions. A succession of steps, formed by the substances in the water which had become hardened, led up to it, ornamented with bead and shell work; while large masses, shaped like cauliflowers or spongy-formed corals, projected from the walls. Out of this curious structure, as I was passing it, shot a column of water sixty feet or more in height, vast volumes of steam escaping at the same time.

It seems curious that I should have been able to remark these objects at a time when my mind was occupied by a matter of so much importance. Still I could not avoid seeing the objects; and although I did not at the time think much about them, they stamped their impression on my mind as I went along. Suddenly two figures appeared, which put every other object out of my sight. My eyes were fixed upon them; I had no doubt that they were Manley and Sergeant Custis. I shouted. They saw and heard me, and came hurrying forward, and we were soon warmly shaking hands.

"Ralph, my dear fellow! we feared that you were lost," exclaimed Manley, "and we have been hunting for you day after day. How haggard you look! How did you manage to lose us? and what has become of your rifle?"

These and numerous other questions I had briefly to answer. How they had missed me, they could not very clearly tell. Instead, however, of coming westward, they had for some time hunted about in the very neighbourhood where they had at first lost sight of me. At length they reached one of my camps, and from thence they had followed me up, although they had been compelled, as I had, to take shelter during the storm.

Of course, they were as much delighted as I was with the extraordinary region in which we found ourselves; and I could now enjoy an examination of its wonders far more than I did at first.

We were very anxious to push on, in order to carry relief to our friends, and to punish the Arrapahas for their audacious raid on our territory, but that evening we could proceed no farther. We therefore cut up the deer, and carried as much of its flesh as we required to camp, where we built a hut, and employed the evening in preparing the venison for the remainder of our journey—for we had snowy heights to surmount, where we might be unable to meet with game. An abundant meal and a night's rest completely set me up; and my friends insisting on alternately keeping watch, I was allowed to sleep on without interruption.

I must pass rapidly over the next few days of our journey. We worked our way along the rugged gorges through which the river forced a passage, and we had torrents to cross, precipitous mountains to climb, amid glaciers and masses of snow, where by a false step we should have been hurled to destruction. But we were mercifully preserved.

Game in these wild regions is scarce, and we were frequently hard pressed for food. In one of the valleys, at the beginning of this part of our journey, nowhere was a drop of drinkable water to be found. For hours we walked on, with bright fountains bubbling up on every side; but they were scalding hot, or so impregnated with minerals that we dared not touch them. Our fate promised to be like that of Tantalus: with water on every side, we were dying of thirst. At length I espied, high up on the mountain slope, a little green oasis, scarcely larger than a small dinner-plate. I scrambled up to it, and, putting down my hand, found a fountain of cool bright water issuing forth. I shouted to my companions, who quickly joined me. Never was nectar drank with more delight; and, revived and strengthened, we again pushed on.

Sometimes we slept in caverns, sometimes in huts built of clods and boughs. Frequently we had to camp on the bare ground, without shelter, our feet as close to the fire as we could venture to place them without running the risk of their being scorched.

At last, to our great joy, we saw the western plains stretching out before us. I call them the plains, although hills of all heights rose in their midst. Far away to the south-west was the great Salt Lake; while in front of us were the mountainous regions bordering the Pacific,—California and its newly-discovered gold-mines. Now descending steep slopes, now traversing gorges, now climbing down precipices, now following the course of a rapid stream, we ultimately reached level ground, and at last arrived at Fort Harwood.

"Why, Broadstreet, my dear fellow!" exclaimed the commandant, who, with a number of other officers, came out on seeing us approach, "we had given you up as lost! Some emigrants who escaped from a train which was attacked reported that every white man on the other side of the pass, for miles to the southward, had been murdered. They had heard, also, that an officer and his men had been cut off, so we naturally concluded you were the unhappy individual."

"Such would have been our fate, if we had attempted to get through the pass; but, guided by my friend here, we crossed the mountain, for the purpose of asking you to send a force of sufficient strength to drive back the Indians, with their rascally white allies," answered the lieutenant.

"The very thing I purposed doing, if I could obtain a trustworthy guide," said the commandant.

"You could not have a more trustworthy one than my friend, Ralph Middlemore," answered Manley. "He knows the mountains better than any white man we are likely to find; and as for Indians, I would not put confidence in one of them."

Of course, I at once expressed my willingness to undertake the duty proposed; and the expedition was speedily arranged. Our troops may not have had a very military appearance, but the men knew how to handle their rifles, and had had experience in border warfare. We numbered fifty in all, besides the drivers of the baggage horses and mules conveying our provisions and ammunition. All not absolutely necessary encumbrances were dispensed with, our camp equipage consisting of a few iron pots, tin cups, and plates. Lieutenant Broadstreet had command of the party, and he was directed to select a fit site for a new fort in the neighbourhood of Roaring Water, to assist in holding the Arrapahas in check for the future.

Not an hour was lost; and by sunrise, two days after our arrival, we commenced our march. I had advised Manley to let me go ahead with a few of the most experienced men, to act as scouts, that we might ascertain whether the enemy still held the pass; but two days had gone by without any signs of the Indians. The remains of their fires, however, showed that they had been there not long before. At the end of the second day, just as we were about to encamp, I caught sight of two figures coming over the brow of a slight elevation. I rubbed my eyes; was it fancy, or did I really see Klitz and Barney before me, precisely as I had seen them on a previous occasion, when attempting to make their escape from the farm? No doubt about it. There was Barney wheeling a barrow, and Klitz, with a couple of muskets on his shoulder, marching behind him. Had I been inclined to superstition, I might have supposed that I beheld a couple of ghosts, or rather beings of another world; but I was convinced, unless I was the victim of some optical delusion, that the two worthies were there in flesh and blood.

I did what every one should do when there exists any doubt about a matter,—I hastened forward to solve the mystery. No sooner did they see me than Klitz dropped his muskets, and Barney, letting go the handles of his wheel-barrow, stood gazing at me with open eyes and outstretched hands.

"Arrah, now, it's the young masther himself!" exclaimed

Barney; whilst the German uttered an exclamation which I did not comprehend. "Sure, now, we were afther thinking your honour was kilt intirely," continued Barney. "Might I be so bold as to axe where your honour comes from now?"

"Let me inquire where you come from, and how you escaped from the burning house," I said. "Although I am glad to see you, I would rather you had rejoined your regiment."

"Sure, Mister Ralph dear, we were returned as dead, and it would have been sore against our consciences to take sarvice under the circumstances. But your honour was axin' how we escaped. Sure, when I was hunting for the Redskin spy, didn't I find out the root-house. And so, afther matters came to the worst, we got in there, with food enough to last until those thieves who wanted our scalps had taken themselves off. As to cutting our way through the enemy, I knew well enough that would not suit me; for I could not run, and Klitz would have been a mark a mile off. So, when you rushed out, he and I dropped down through the trap and stowed ourselves away. The Indians, marcifully, niver came to look for us. In truth, while they were hunting about down came the building on their heads, and we could hear their shrieks and cries as they tried to scramble out from among the flames. If it had not been for a small vent-hole far away up in a corner, we should have been suffocated, maybe. All day long we could hear them screeching and hallooing outside the house; but before night the thieves of the world took themselves off, we suppose, for all was silent.

"At the end of a couple of days we thought we might safely venture to take a few mouthfuls of fresh air, and begin to work our way out from among the ruins. It was no easy job, but we got free at last. Neither Redskin nor white man was to be seen; and of all the buildings, the hut and the mill only were standing. The villains had carried off all our blankets and most of the cooking-pots, but enough was left for our wants, seeing that we had nothing to put in them. However, Klitz was not the boy to starve. He soon caught some fish, and I got hold of a sheep which came up to the door; and if there had only been a dhrop of the cratur', we should have lived like princes. One thing there was which the Indians had not carried off, and that was a wheel-barrow. When Klitz saw it, 'We will go to California!' says he. Says I, 'I'm the boy for it!' So, as we had our muskets and a few rounds of ammunition, afther drying the mutton and making some other necessary preparations we set off. The Indians had left the country, and no one stopped us, so surely your honour won't be so hard as to stop us now!"

"That must depend on what Lieutenant Broadstreet has to say in the matter," I observed. "I am under his orders, and will conduct you to him."

Klitz elongated his visage on hearing this, but Barney took the matter with his usual good-humour.

In consideration of the dangers the men had gone through, and their conduct in the defence of the farm, the lieutenant treated them kindly. He could not allow them to continue on their way to California, of course, which they most certainly would never have reached, but he inflicted no greater punishment than ordering them to mount the baggage-mules and return with us.

We did not entirely rely on Barney's report that the Indians had left the neighbourhood, though it perhaps made us less cautious than we would otherwise have been. As I was well-mounted, I frequently went on a considerable distance ahead, eager to fall in with some one from whom I might gain intelligence of Uncle Jeff, Clarice, or our friends. I did not suppose that Uncle Jeff would remain in the mountains where we had left him, but that he would certainly have come down to meet us; or perhaps, should Bartle and Gideon have escaped, he might have rejoined them and returned to Roaring Water.

We had got through the pass, and were about to march to the southward, in the hope of overtaking the enemy, should they be still lingering in that part of the country, when I saw smoke ascending from the level ground close to the foot of the mountain, and some way ahead. On watching it, I was satisfied that it rose from an encampment of white or red men. As there was little doubt that information could be obtained from the inhabitants, whoever they were, the sergeant and I, with two well-mounted troopers, rode forward, keeping on the alert to guard against coming suddenly on an enemy.

As we got nearer, I saw, by means of a telescope which I had obtained at the fort, an Indian camp of a more permanent character than I had yet fallen in with in that neighbourhood. This was a proof that the inhabitants were friendly.

In a short time several persons appeared; and on seeing us one of them came forward, habited in the costume of a chief, a quiver at his back and a bow in his hand. A squaw followed him. He stopped and gazed at me. Then, as I rode on, he advanced, and, putting out his hand, exclaimed—

"You know me!—Piomingo. This my squaw, you save my life and her life, and I am ever your friend."

I told him that I was very glad to see him, and that he could give me information I very much desired. In the course of conversation he informed me that he had talked with Winnemak, and had buried, as he said, the war-hatchet; and he had therefore come and settled in that district. He had also preserved my horse with the greatest care; and, he added, he was ready to restore him to me in good condition. With regard to Uncle Jeff, he could tell me nothing. As my uncle, however, had not rejoined Winnemak, I concluded that the latter was still in the mountains, well contented with his new locality, and engaged in shooting and trapping.

"Can you give me any information about my other friends?" I asked.

One white man, he said, had gone to Winnemak's camp; and from his description I had little doubt that the person he spoke of was either Bartle or Gideon. I was very sure, however, that either of them would without delay have rejoined Uncle Jeff. What Piomingo told me about the other caused me much anxiety. He had been captured by the Arrapahas, he said, who had carried him about with them; probably, according to their cruel custom, with the intention of ultimately putting him to death in some barbarous manner.

As Piomingo volunteered to lead a party of us in search of the marauders, who still had, according to his report, a white man with them, I at once accepted his offer, and would gladly have set off immediately; but it was important first to carry assistance to Uncle Jeff and Clarice, who could not fail—so Manley thought—to require it. He and I, with twenty troopers and some of our baggage animals, accordingly turned to the northward, leaving Sergeant Custis and the remainder of our force to watch the pass, in order to prevent the return of the Arrapahas.

We pushed on as fast as our horses would go, the lieutenant being fully as eager as I was, but it took as two days to reach the foot of the mountains. Manley declared that he could not have found the spot had it not been for my assistance. We here formed camp, while he and I, with six of our strongest baggage animals, and men to look after them, took our way up the mountain.

I need scarcely describe the route. Sometimes we made tolerable progress, at other times we had to use the greatest caution to escape falling over the precipices which we had now on one side, now on the other. But the most arduous part of the undertaking was forcing our way through the primeval forests, over trunks of trees, and through pools of water, into which the horses sank up to their knees. The poor brutes had an uncomfortable time of it. The men, armed with thick sticks, went behind whacking them unmercifully, while others dragged away at their heads. I was thankful to have the task of acting as guide, although it was not an easy one—having every now and then to climb over fallen logs or leap across pools. I was, however, saved the pain of witnessing the sufferings of the animals; and I determined, if possible, to find an easier path down again.

At length a height which separated us from the first valley was passed; and looking down, to our infinite satisfaction we caught sight of a well-constructed hut, with a wreath of smoke ascending from its chimney. All, then, was likely to be well. Manley and I, leaving our men to follow with the animals, hurried down, and in less than a quarter of an hour we were shaking hands with Uncle Jeff and Clarice. I need scarcely describe how Manley and my fair young sister met, but it was very evident that they were not sorry to see each other. Rachel came out, beaming with smiles; and in a short time Pat Sperry appeared, followed by another person whom I was truly glad to see—Gideon Tuttle. The latter had joined Uncle Jeff some days before. Although desperately wounded, he had managed to make his escape, and had lain in hiding in the mountains for several days, till he had recovered sufficient strength to travel. The report he gave us of Bartle, however, was truly alarming. There could be no doubt that he had been captured by the Indians, and, Gideon feared, must have been put to death by them; but when I told him what Piomingo said, he became more hopeful as to the fate of his old friend.

"If he is alive, we will find him out, wherever he may be!" he exclaimed. "Even if the varmints have him in the middle of their camp, we will manage to set him free."

Uncle Jeff, as I expected, had not been idle. Ever since the day we had left him, he had been hunting and trapping, and had collected a large store of skins of all sorts of animals, with dried meat enough to supply an army. The baggage animals we had brought could carry but a small amount of the stores collected by Uncle Jeff. It was arranged, therefore, that a larger number should be sent up as soon as possible, to bring away the remainder. Who was to take charge of them? was the question. Uncle Jeff, Gideon, and I, were naturally anxious to return to Roaring Water, that we might get up huts and re-establish ourselves before the commencement of winter.

While we were in this dilemma, Winnemak and several of his braves appeared. On hearing of our difficulty, he said, "Commit them to my care. I will protect them with my life—although I believe no one will venture up here to carry them off. I have, as yet, had few opportunities of showing my gratitude. I failed to assist you, when I wished to do so, against the Arrapahas; but in this matter I can, at all events, render you a service."

"Where will Maysotta remain while you are up in the mountains?" asked Uncle Jeff, after he had accepted Winnemak's offer.

"Oh, let her come with us!" exclaimed Clarice. "I wish to

show her that I am grateful for the service which she rendered me; and she may perhaps be pleased with the life we lead. She has several times expressed a wish to know how white people spend their time."

The chief, who seldom interfered with the movements of his daughter, replied that she was at liberty to do as she wished, and that we should find her in the camp at the foot of the mountains.

Lieutenant Broadstreet had to rejoin his men as soon as possible, and no time, therefore, was lost in commencing our journey down the mountain. Winnemak and several of his people were left in charge of Uncle Jeff's hut and stores.

We had not a few difficulties to encounter on our return, but Clarice, by whose side Manley rode whenever the path would permit, endured them bravely; and we ultimately, without accident, reached the foot of the mountains, where we found Maysotta encamped with the remainder of her people. She was well pleased with the proposal Clarice made to her; and her baggage being put into little bulk, she mounted her horse and accompanied us forthwith.

CHAPTER THIRTEEN

ON OUR WAY WE VISIT PIOMINGO—HE TELLS US OF BARTLE'S CAPTIVITY, AND OFFERS TO ASSIST US IN HIS RECOVERY—GIDEON, PIOMINGO, AND I SET OUT, FOLLOWED BY A STRONG PARTY UNDER SERGEANT CUSTIS—WE DISCOVER THE TRAIL, AND FOLLOW IT UP—HORRIBLE CRUELTIES PRACTISED BY INDIANS ON THEIR PRISONERS—THE TRAIL LEADS ALONG THE MOUNTAIN—WE SEE A FIGURE ABOVE US—IT IS BARTLE—IS HE ALIVE?—JUST IN TIME—GIDEON AND I STAY BY HIM—I AFTERWARDS SET OFF TO OBTAIN HELP—PIOMINGO HAS SENT A LETTER—WE ARRIVE SAFE AT ROARING WATER—HARD AT WORK REBUILDING THE HOUSE—A FORT ESTABLISHED—BARNEY AND KLITZ JOIN US—A VISIT FROM MANLEY—A PROPOSAL, AND CONFESSION—UNCLE JEFF APPROVES OF THE ENGAGEMENT OF MANLEY AND CLARICE—WINNEMAK AND PIOMINGO BECOME CHRISTIANS, AND INSTRUCT THEIR PEOPLE—THE HOUSE REBUILT—SETTLERS GATHER ROUND US, AND UNCLE JEFF'S FARM BECOMES THE MOST FLOURISHING IN THE NEIGHBOURHOOD.

As we approached Piomingo's camp, or rather village, we saw him hurrying out to meet us.

"I have gained information for you," he said, "about one of your white friends who has long been held in captivity by the Arrapahas. The party who have him remained for some time in the neighbourhood of Roaring Water, if they are not there still. If you hasten on, you may overtake them; but it would be dangerous to approach with a large band, in case they should immediately kill their prisoner—they have already killed several who had fallen into their power—rather than run the risk of allowing him to escape. My advice is, that a small number of experienced men should pursue them, followed by a larger party at a short distance; and I willingly offer to serve as a scout to accompany the first party. If we can find the Arrapahas in camp, we may be able to liberate the prisoner; or if we can form an ambush and pounce suddenly out on them, we may manage to cut the thongs with which he is bound, mount him on one of our horses, and carry him off."

As we were convinced that the white man of whom Piomingo spoke was Bartle Won, Uncle Jeff and Gideon accepted the brave's offer without hesitation. It was finally settled that Piomingo, Gideon, and I should push on until we came upon the trail of the Arrapahas, and that a party of twenty men, under Sergeant Custis, should follow us. We were then cautiously to approach the camp of the enemy, and endeavour by some means or other to liberate Bartle. We had confidence in the success of our plan, for Piomingo had ever been celebrated for his cunning and audacity, which he had in times past exercised in less reputable ways than that in which he now proposed to employ them. Some of Winnemak and Piomingo's people, who were now on good terms, scoured the country as scouts; and from the reports they brought us we were satisfied that the chief body of the enemy had completely deserted the neighbourhood. Still, the party of whom Piomingo had heard might have remained behind, and we therefore at once commenced our search for their trail.

But I must be brief in my account. For two days we searched in every direction, scarcely resting, till at length we discovered a trail which Piomingo was confident was that of our foes; and, moreover, he said they had a white man with them. They had, however, he thought, passed some days before. Piomingo sent back one of his men to urge Sergeant Custis to come on rapidly; and we pushed forward as fast as we could travel, hoping soon to overtake the Arrapahas.

After following the trail, we found that it took the way along the mountains. This was rather an advantage in some respects, as, being accustomed to mountain travelling, we might move on faster than those of whom we were in pursuit. As, however, we were made of flesh and blood, we were obliged to encamp at night, although the dawn of day found us again in pursuit.

Piomingo thrilled my heart with horror by an account which he gave of the cruelties practised by the savages on some of their captives, and I had great fear that our friend Bartle might have been subjected to the same horrible tortures. Piomingo told us that he himself had been present at some of the scenes he described. It showed me how debased men, formed in the image of God, can become, when they have departed from Him, and how cruel by nature is the human heart, which can devise and take satisfaction in the infliction of such barbarities. The white men who were thus treated had done nothing to injure the Indians, except in attempting to defend their lives and property when attacked. The captives having been brought out into an open space, bound hand and foot, the Indians threw off their usual garments, and dressed themselves in the most fantastic manner. One of their victims was first led forward and stretched on the ground, to which he was bound by cords and pegs, so that he could move none of his limbs. The savages then commenced a wild dance round him, jeering and mocking him, while they described the various tortures for which he must be prepared. One of the unfortunate victim's companions was, in the meantime, held, with his hands bound behind him, and made a witness to his sufferings. The savages, as they danced round and round him, stooped down and pricked him with daggers and knives, taking good care not to wound him mortally. Next one of the wretches, seizing his knife, cut his scalp from off his head; while others brought some burning embers of wood and placed them on his breast.

But I see no advantage in further mentioning the diabolical cruelties practised by these savages of which Piomingo told us. Far removed from the benign influences of Christianity, these red men only acted according to the impulses of their barbarous nature. The thought came upon me with great force, Is it not the duty of white men who are Christians to send the blessed light of the gospel, by every means in their power, to their benighted fellow-creatures? They have souls as we have, and they are as capable of receiving the truths of the gospel as we are. Bold, energetic men, imbued with the love of souls, are required, who, ready to sacrifice all the enjoyments of civilisation, will cast themselves fearlessly among the native tribes, and by patience and perseverance endeavour to induce them to listen to the message of reconciliation, and to imitate the example of Him who died for them.

I spoke earnestly and faithfully to Piomingo of this, and I was thankful to find that he listened not only willingly but eagerly to what I said.

"Yes," he exclaimed at length, "I see that you are right. Although some white men have set us a bad example, it is no reason that all should do so. The truths about which you speak are independent of man. There must be bad white men as well as bad red men; but I am sure that those who follow the example of Him of whom you tell me, the Son of the Great Spirit, must be good men. I will try to follow him, and when we get back, you must tell me more about him."

I gladly promised to do so, and was thankful for this opportunity of speaking to Piomingo.

Before starting next morning we sent a message to the sergeant, begging him to keep as close to the foot of the mountain as possible, as we were sure the enemy could not have gone far up; indeed, their trail led along the lower part of the side. They had taken this direction, probably, in order that they might obtain a view over the plain, and thus the more easily escape from those who by this time, they must have known through their scouts, were in pursuit of them, although they could not be aware that our small party was so close at their heels. In a few hours more, we believed, we should probably be up with them; and we hoped that while they were in camp we might find some means or other of releasing Bartle.

Though generally keeping our eyes ahead, or down on the plain, I happened on one occasion to look up the mountain. On the height above me was the figure of a human being. I pointed it out to my companions.

"There is no doubt about it," exclaimed Gideon; "what you see is a cross, with a man, well-nigh stripped, bound to it."

The spot was one difficult of access, but it had been reached shortly before, and, Piomingo declared, by Indians, whose trail he discovered on the hard rock, where Gideon and I could not perceive the slightest marks.

"That is Bartle," cried Gideon as we were climbing on. "Little chance, however, of the poor fellow being alive. The cruel varmints! I'll punish them one of these days for what they have done."

The expressions which his indignation drew forth were very natural, but they were not in accordance with the precepts I had been endeavouring to inculcate on Piomingo.

As we hastened on Gideon cried, "I think I saw his head move; if so, he must be alive. We are coming! cheer up, cheer up, Bartle; we are coming to your help!" he shouted.

The faint sound of a human voice was heard in return.

"He is alive," I exclaimed; "he is alive!" and I waved my cap as we rushed to our friend's assistance.

Another minute, and we were by Bartle's side. We could perceive no wound, but his eyes were starting from his head, and his tongue protruded. Not a moment was lost in cutting the lashings with which he was bound to the stump of a small tree, with another rough piece of wood fastened across it. A few minutes later, and I believe he would have breathed his last. We had fortunately brought with us a bottle of water and some spirits, some of which we poured down his throat, and in a wonderfully short time he revived, and was able to tell us what had happened to him. He had rendered one of his captors a service on some occasion, and this man had sufficient influence with the others to preserve his life. When, however, they found themselves closely pursued by our troops, they were about to kill him; but, at the instigation of the brave who had hitherto saved him from being put to death, they resolved to bind him to the tree and leave him. In all likelihood, his friend had proposed this with the intention of afterwards returning and setting him free.

As Bartle would certainly be unable to move for some time, Gideon and I remained by him, while Piomingo returned to inform Sergeant Custis of our success, and also to warn him that the enemy were not far ahead. The sergeant, we afterwards heard, pushed rapidly on, and in a short time came up with the party, and, by the careful way in which he approached, took them completely by surprise. They attempted to defend themselves, but the greater number were cut to pieces—a few only escaping to the southward.

Gideon and I, I have said, had been left on the mountain-side to look after Bartle. The first thing Gideon did was to take off his own coat and wrap it round our friend, whose limbs were swollen by the pressure of the cords, while he was chilled by long exposure to the cold air; indeed, most men would have sunk under the sufferings he had endured. How were we to get him down the mountain? was the next question. He could not walk, and Gideon and I together were unable to carry him. The spot was exposed to a hot sun by day, and to cold winds by night, and there were no materials at hand to build a hut; indeed, but little wood even to form a fire. At last I proposed setting off to try and obtain help,—though, should the troops or the Indians who accompanied us have gone south, it might be a long time before I could fall in with any one. There was nothing else to be done, however, as far as we could see, although I greatly feared that before I could return Bartle would have succumbed.

"Quick, Ralph," said Gideon, as I rose to set off. "Do not forget some food; and bring a litter, or something of that kind, to carry Bartle on."

I had scarcely got a hundred feet down the mountain when I saw two Indians in the distance, coming towards me, each carrying something on his back, and a long pole in his hand. I waved to them, and they made signals in reply. They were soon close to me, and on coming up they said that they had been sent by Piomingo, and that they carried materials for forming a litter. He had thought of the very thing we required. It was rapidly put together; and placing Bartle on it, we each of us took the end of a pole, and began cautiously to descend the mountain. Of necessity our progress was very slow. Sometimes we had to place the litter on the ground, not for the sake of resting ourselves, but that we might lower it with more caution. Thus proceeding, we at last reached the plain, where, as the day had closed, we encamped.

Next morning, Bartle, although better, was still unable to walk; we therefore carried him the whole way to Roaring Water. We found Uncle Jeff standing in the midst of the ruins of the old house,—in no desponding mood, however,—and he welcomed Bartle as he would have done a beloved brother.

"You will soon come round, Bartle," he said, as he took his hand; "and we will get a house up as big and as strong as the old one."

"Ay! that we will," answered Bartle; "and if the Redskins pay us another visit, we will take good care that they shall never get inside it."

* * * * *

The hut had been thoroughly cleaned out, and Clarice, Maysotta, and Rachel had taken possession of it, while the rest of the party occupied the mill.

Lieutenant Broadstreet had, in the meantime, fixed on a good site for a fort on the summit of a precipice by the river-side, and his men were busily engaged in cutting and filing up the palisades which were to surround it. So much was he occupied in the duty he had to perform, that he could rarely come over to Roaring Water; while I was so fully employed that I had no time to visit him.

We were greatly in want of labourers to supply the places of the poor fellows who had been killed when the Indians attacked the house, and at last Uncle Jeff told me to go over to the fort and ascertain if any men were likely to obtain their discharge, and if so, to offer them good wages.

"You can tell the lieutenant that we shall be glad to see him over here whenever he can come," said Uncle Jeff, "although we have not the best accommodation in the world to offer him."

I had little doubt that Manley would not be influenced by the latter consideration; so, mounting my horse, I rode off to the fort, and gave him Uncle Jeff's message.

"I can afford you two hands, at all events," he answered, and I saw a twinkle in his eyes. "They know the place, and perhaps you may get more work out of them than I can; only take care they do not run away."

I guessed to whom he alluded; nor was I mistaken. We went out together, and he summoned Klitz and Barney, who were slowly working away with pick, axe, and spade.

"Men," he said, "you have claimed your discharge; you shall have it, if you are willing to go and take service at Roaring Water."

"Sure, with the greatest pleasure in me life; there's not a finer gintleman on this side of the Atlantic than Mr Crockett," said Barney.

Klitz simply gave a grunt of acquiescence.

The whole matter was arranged; and they were to return with me the next day. I was also glad to obtain two more men, who, though they belonged to that class of individuals known, as "Uncle Sam's bad bargains," and might be lazy rascals when labouring for a Government for which they did not care a cent, turned out to be very ready to serve a master who treated them kindly and paid them well. As we travelled along they showed no inclination to decamp, but chatted and laughed, each in his own style—Barney being undoubtedly the leading wit of the party. They were heartily welcome at Roaring Water, and both Klitz and Barney showed that they were willing and able to work. The only thing which seemed to put the German out was when any allusion was made to a wheel-barrow.

We had just begun active operations when Winnemak came to see his daughter. Maysotta, however, had no inclination to return with him, and begged that she might remain to assist her new friend, from whom she was hearing more wonderful things daily, as well as gaining more knowledge. Winnemak offered us the services of some of his men, who were willing to work for wages; and although they were not equal to the worst of the white men, yet, by Uncle Jeff's good management, they were made very useful.

From some passing emigrant trains we obtained a good supply of tools,—axes and saws,—and we were busily at work from sunrise to sunset. Clarice and Rachel had succeeded in recovering some of the cattle, pigs, and poultry which had strayed, and in a short time the farm began to assume something of its former appearance.

I had, one afternoon, come back from the forest in which we obtained our timber, in order to get a fresh axe in place of one which I had broken, when I found Maysotta alone in the hut. On asking for Clarice, I was told she had gone to the cool fountain for a pitcher of water. It struck me that something was amiss with the Indian girl, but what it was I could not tell I was going on to the mill, where I expected to find an axe, when Maysotta added—

"The young white chief, from the fort out there, came here just now inquiring for you. When he heard that Clarice was at the spring, he hastened off in that direction, without seeming to regard me."

Having obtained the axe, I set off after Manley, whom I was anxious to see, and as I got near the spring I heard him in conversation with my sister.

"Oh no, no! I must not leave my uncle and Ralph; I should be neglecting my duty, should I do so," said Clarice.

"But I have told you how devotedly, how fondly I love you," said Manley. "Do you not love me in return?"

"Yes, I do; I have loved no one else," she replied.

On hearing this confession I should have withdrawn, for I had perfect confidence in Manley, and what I had heard gave me unbounded satisfaction. Clarice, however, had heard me moving among the bushes, and turned her eyes towards me with a startled look. I was sure she had perceived me, so I at once came forward. Manley put out his hand.

"You heard what I said to your sister?"

"Yes; and what she said in reply," I answered. "It gives me the greatest possible pleasure. There is no man I ever met whom I should so much like as a brother-in-law. I would advise Clarice to tell Uncle Jeff at once, and hear what he says about the matter. My belief is, that he will not say anything which either of you would dislike."

Dear little Clarice looked very happy when I said this. I was not surprised that Manley had fallen desperately in love with her, although her beauty certainly did not depend on the elegance of her costume, for she had come out without shoes or stockings, with her hair hanging down over her shoulders, and in her rough working-dress. I must confess I forgot all about my axe, and where I had been going; and having been taken into the confidence of Manley and my sister, I remained talking with them, and settling plans for the future. Suddenly, however, I recollected that I had work to do; and I had an idea that the young couple would not object just then to my attending to my duties. At all events, they said nothing to detain me. Manley agreed to remain with us that night, and I advised him to lose no time in speaking to Uncle Jeff.

To make a long story short, when Uncle Jeff came back after his day's work, Manley, following my advice, spoke to him. His reply was what I had expected:—

"You shall have her with all my heart, for I am very sure you will make her a good husband."

Manley had received his appointment as commandant of the fort; but as the buildings were not as yet fully completed, nor would be fit for a lady's reception during the winter, it was settled that the young couple should wait until next spring to be married, when it was hoped that the chaplain at Fort Harwood would be able to come over and perform the ceremony.

Before the winter set in we had got up a sufficient portion of the house for our accommodation, while the new field hands occupied the hut. Our friend Winnemak paid us frequent visits, too, always bringing a supply of game, which was very welcome, as we had but little time for hunting, and were unwilling to kill any of our farm-stock.

Maysotta had always much to say to her father, and he willingly allowed her to remain with us. His mind was already beginning to awaken to spiritual truth, as he had had the gospel explained to him, and he now compared it with the dark heathen superstitions in which he had hitherto believed. Maysotta entreated Clarice to tell her father all she had told her. She gladly did so, and the hitherto proud chief "became as a little child." He at last fixed his camp in our neighbourhood, and used to visit us nearly every day, in order that he might receive instruction. He even expressed a wish to learn to read; so Uncle Jeff and I became his masters, aided occasionally by Clarice and Maysotta, who had already made considerable progress. The chief's memory was wonderfully good, too, and he thus rapidly learned whole chapters of the Bible, from a translation which we had obtained in the dialect of his people. His great desire was now not only to learn himself, but to induce his own people to accept the blessings of the gospel; and as his wish was to imitate us in everything, he had put up a log-house of considerable size in his village.

I had often promised to pay him a visit. One Sunday I had ridden over to the fort, after Clarice's marriage, to see her and join the service there, when on my way back I bethought me of my promise to Winnemak. I accordingly rode to his village. None of his men were about; so, fastening up my horse, I went towards his house. As I looked in at the door, I saw him standing up at one end, while his chief men and braves were seated around him, attentively listening to the words which fell from his lips. Once he would have addressed them only on some warlike or political matter, but now he was preaching the blessed gospel, while those fierce warriors sat listening with the most profound attention to his words.

What were those words? He was telling them that they must become as children; that they must be born again, that their old evil nature might be overcome; that they must do good to their enemies, and forgive those who should injure them; that they must lead pure and holy lives, not giving way to their angry feelings, or even indulging in angry thoughts. He told them, too, of the Saviour's love, and the Saviour's death; how God would forgive their sins, which, though red as scarlet, would become white as wool, if they trusted that by that death he had taken their sins upon himself, and had become their Saviour, their Advocate, their great High Priest.

Winnemak having thus become a Christian, did not rest content until he had used every effort to convert the whole of his tribe. Nor did he stop here: he went to other tribes; and when he found his own influence was not sufficient, he procured the assistance of white missionaries, whom he supported and protected.

His example was followed by his former enemy Piomingo, whose young wife and himself became industrious settlers—the greater number of their tribe completely abandoning their old barbarous customs. The only regret of Winnemak was that he and his people had not received these glorious tidings in earlier days, before they had almost ceased to exist as a people in the land where once their warriors were counted by thousands.

But I have been anticipating events. From several of the emigrant trains which came by next season, we obtained not only such stores as we required, but several useful hands; while many of the families, seeing the fertility of the country, and the progress we had made, to say nothing of the protection of the military post, resolved, instead of incurring the dangers of a longer journey, to settle in our neighbourhood.

The new house, as Uncle Jeff and Bartle intended, was far superior to the old one, and although we hoped that we should never again be attacked, yet it was built with an eye to defence, and was considered almost as strong as the fort itself. Happily, however, we have never had occasion to try its capabilities of withstanding a siege.

Fields were added to fields; the stock increased; and God prospering us notwithstanding the heavy losses we had incurred, Uncle Jeff's farm eventually became the most nourishing in the neighbourhood.

ABOUT THE AUTHOR

William Henry Giles Kingston (1814 - 1880), writer of tales for boys, born in London, but spent much of his youth in Oporto, where his father was a merchant.

His first book, The Circassian Chief, appeared in 1844. His first book for boys, Peter the Whaler, was published in 1851, and had such success that he retired from business and devoted himself entirely to the production of this kind of literature, in which his popularity was deservedly great; and during 30 years he wrote upwards of 130 tales, including The Three Midshipmen (1862), The Three Lieutenants (1874), The Three Commanders (1875), The Three Admirals (1877), Digby Heathcote, etc.

He also conducted various papers, including The Colonist, and Colonial Magazine and East India Review. He was also interested in emigration, volunteering, and various philanthropic schemes. For services in negotiating a commercial treaty with Portugal he received a Portuguese knighthood, and for his literary labours a Government pension.

Friedrich Kerst
Friedrich Nietzsche
Fyodor Dostoyevsky
G.A. Henty
G.K. Chesterton
Gabrielle E. Jackson
Garrett P. Serviss
Gaston Leroux
George A. Warren
George Ade
Geroge Bernard Shaw
George Cary Eggleston
George Durston
George Ebers
George Eliot
George Gissing
George MacDonald
George Meredith
George Orwell
George Sylvester Viereck
George Tucker
George W. Cable
George Wharton James
Gertrude Atherton
Gordon Casserly
Grace E. King
Grace Gallatin
Grace Greenwood
Grant Allen
Guillermo A. Sherwell
Gulielma Zollinger
Gustav Flaubert
H. A. Cody
H. B. Irving
H.C. Bailey
H. G. Wells
H. H. Munro
H. Irving Hancock
H. R. Naylor
H. Rider Haggard
H. W. C. Davis
Haldeman Julius
Hall Caine
Hamilton Wright Mabie
Hans Christian Andersen
Harold Avery
Harold McGrath
Harriet Beecher Stowe
Harry Castlemon
Harry Coghill
Harry Houidini

Hayden Carruth
Helent Hunt Jackson
Helen Nicolay
Hendrik Conscience
Hendy David Thoreau
Henri Barbusse
Henrik Ibsen
Henry Adams
Henry Ford
Henry Frost
Henry James
Henry Jones Ford
Henry Seton Merriman
Henry W Longfellow
Herbert A. Giles
Herbert Carter
Herbert N. Casson
Herman Hesse
Hildegard G. Frey
Homer
Honore De Balzac
Horace B. Day
Horace Walpole
Horatio Alger Jr.
Howard Pyle
Howard R. Garis
Hugh Lofting
Hugh Walpole
Humphry Ward
Ian Maclaren
Inez Haynes Gillmore
Irving Bacheller
Isabel Cecilia Williams
Isabel Hornibrook
Israel Abrahams
Ivan Turgenev
J.G.Austin
J. Henri Fabre
J. M. Barrie
J. M. Walsh
J. Macdonald Oxley
J. R. Miller
J. S. Fletcher
J. S. Knowles
J. Storer Clouston
J. W. Duffield
Jack London
Jacob Abbott
James Allen
James Andrews
James Baldwin

James Branch Cabell
James DeMille
James Joyce
James Lane Allen
James Lane Allen
James Oliver Curwood
James Oppenheim
James Otis
James R. Driscoll
Jane Abbott
Jane Austen
Jane L. Stewart
Janet Aldridge
Jens Peter Jacobsen
Jerome K. Jerome
Jessie Graham Flower
John Buchan
John Burroughs
John Cournos
John F. Kennedy
John Gay
John Glasworthy
John Habberton
John Joy Bell
John Kendrick Bangs
John Milton
John Philip Sousa
John Taintor Foote
Jonas Lauritz Idemil Lie
Jonathan Swift
Joseph A. Altsheler
Joseph Carey
Joseph Conrad
Joseph E. Badger Jr
Joseph Hergesheimer
Joseph Jacobs
Jules Vernes
Julian Hawthrone
Julie A Lippmann
Justin Huntly McCarthy
Kakuzo Okakura
Karle Wilson Baker
Kate Chopin
Kenneth Grahame
Kenneth McGaffey
Kate Langley Bosher
Kate Langley Bosher
Katherine Cecil Thurston
Katherine Stokes
L. A. Abbot
L. T. Meade

L. Frank Baum
Latta Griswold
Laura Dent Crane
Laura Lee Hope
Laurence Housman
Lawrence Beasley
Leo Tolstoy
Leonid Andreyev
Lewis Carroll
Lewis Sperry Chafer
Lilian Bell
Lloyd Osbourne
Louis Hughes
Louis Joseph Vance
Louis Tracy
Louisa May Alcott
Lucy Fitch Perkins
Lucy Maud Montgomery
Luther Benson
Lydia Miller Middleton
Lyndon Orr
M. Corvus
M. H. Adams
Margaret E. Sangster
Margret Howth
Margaret Vandercook
Margaret W. Hungerford
Margret Penrose
Maria Edgeworth
Maria Thompson Daviess
Mariano Azuela
Marion Polk Angellotti
Mark Overton
Mark Twain
Mary Austin
Mary Catherine Crowley
Mary Cole
Mary Hastings Bradley
Mary Roberts Rinehart
Mary Rowlandson
M. Wollstonecraft Shelley
Maud Lindsay
Max Beerbohm
Myra Kelly
Nathaniel Hawthrone
Nicolo Machiavelli
O. F. Walton
Oscar Wilde

Owen Johnson
P.G. Wodehouse
Paul and Mabel Thorne
Paul G. Tomlinson
Paul Severing
Percy Brebner
Percy Keese Fitzhugh
Peter B. Kyne
Plato
Quincy Allen
R. Derby Holmes
R. L. Stevenson
R. S. Ball
Rabindranath Tagore
Rahul Alvares
Ralph Bonehill
Ralph Henry Barbour
Ralph Victor
Ralph Waldo Emmerson
Rene Descartes
Ray Cummings
Rex Beach
Rex E. Beach
Richard Harding Davis
Richard Jefferies
Richard Le Gallienne
Robert Barr
Robert Frost
Robert Gordon Anderson
Robert L. Drake
Robert Lansing
Robert Lynd
Robert Michael Ballantyne
Robert W. Chambers
Rosa Nouchette Carey
Rudyard Kipling
Saint Augustine
Samuel B. Allison
Samuel Hopkins Adams
Sarah Bernhardt
Sarah C. Hallowell
Selma Lagerlof
Sherwood Anderson
Sigmund Freud
Standish O'Grady
Stanley Weyman
Stella Benson
Stella M. Francis

Stephen Crane
Stewart Edward White
Stijn Streuvels
Swami Abhedananda
Swami Parmananda
T. S. Ackland
T. S. Arthur
The Princess Der Ling
Thomas A. Janvier
Thomas A Kempis
Thomas Anderton
Thomas Bailey Aldrich
Thomas Bulfinch
Thomas De Quincey
Thomas Dixon
Thomas H. Huxley
Thomas Hardy
Thomas More
Thornton W. Burgess
U. S. Grant
Upton Sinclair
Valentine Williams
Various Authors
Vaughan Kester
Victor Appleton
Victor G. Durham
Victoria Cross
Virginia Woolf
Wadsworth Camp
Walter Camp
Walter Scott
Washington Irving
Wilbur Lawton
Wilkie Collins
Willa Cather
Willard F. Baker
William Dean Howells
William le Queux
W. Makepeace Thackeray
William W. Walter
William Shakespeare
Winston Churchill
Yei Theodora Ozaki
Yogi Ramacharaka
Young E. Allison
Zane Grey

www.ingramcontent.com/pod-product-compliance
Lightning Source LLC
Chambersburg PA
CBHW020551310726
48979CB00008B/1174/J

* 9 7 8 1 4 2 1 8 4 7 7 3 3 *